Happiness, God, and Man

Christoph Cardinal Schönborn

Happiness, God, and Man

Edited by Hubert Philipp Weber

Translated by Michael J. Miller

IGNATIUS PRESS   SAN FRANCISCO

Original German edition:
Vom geglückten Leben
© 2008 by Amalthea Signum Verlag, Vienna

Main cover image:
Creation of Adam by Michelangelo (detail)
Sistine Chapel, Vatican
© istockphoto/estelle75

Cover design by Roxanne Mei Lum

ISBN 978-1-58617-361-6
Library of Congress Control Number 2010931416
Printed in the United States of America ⊗

Contents

6

III. MAN

IV. REMEMBERING THE TERROR

V. LITERATURE

Introduction

All men want to be happy. The longing for happiness does not have to be learned; it is "innate". And it can hardly be unlearned. For we never simply acquiesce in unhappiness. Christian faith, the Christian way of life, and the imitation of Christ are understood to be signposts pointing the way to happiness. Therein lies their attractiveness; upon this depends their credibility.

Although the texts collected in this book were composed on very dissimilar occasions, they all revolve around the central theme of what makes life happy. They also document the personal search and longing for the happiness that God has promised and that so often is glimpsed only in its counterpart—the experience of suffering.

Part 1 is explicitly concerned with man's striving for happiness and his experiences of happiness, small and great. Thomas Aquinas sees friendship as the expression of the love that makes us happy. Friendship with God is possible, and it is the greatest happiness imaginable, although often it is still so distant.

Part 2 deals first with the revelation of God's name in the Bible. His closeness and his mercy are the original promises of happiness. Next come two Lenten homilies that the late Cardinal Lustiger invited me to preach at Notre Dame Cathedral in Paris. The first one addresses the apparent contradiction in the fact that Jesus singles out unhappy people, the sorrowful, as being blessed. The second one asks how Europe can rediscover itself today, so that it does not remain without hope.

Part 3 contains homilies that were preached at liturgies for four Austrian celebrities. First comes a tribute to Otto von Habsburg, son of the last Austrian emperor, Blessed Karl of Austria. Three funeral homilies follow. I gave the first for my predecessor's predecessor, Franz Cardinal König, at his Requiem Mass in 2004. Pope John Paul II had sent Joseph Cardinal Ratzinger—who today is our Holy Father, Pope Benedict XVI—to attend the Mass as his personal representative. My homily at the funeral Mass for Austrian President Thomas Klestil elicited a major response for several reasons, probably because I so openly addressed his painful failure in marriage, his longing for a happy life, as well as his (and the Church's) need to deal with it properly. Nor could the homily at the funeral Mass for former Austrian President Kurt Waldheim fail to mention the drama that he had to go through, despite all efforts to achieve reconciliation.

The great drama, the tragedy of the twentieth century is the subject of *part 4*. Ideologies promised great happiness on earth. In order to bring it about, they maintained, one had to do away with whatever or whoever was hindering the arrival of that happiness. Two speeches, given in Mauthausen and in Yad Vashem in Jerusalem, testify to the devastating consequences of those ideologies.

Finally, *part 5* is dedicated to literature. I admit that I am a fan of Gertrud von Le Fort and C. S. Lewis. Both authors, as I see their works, give witness to a happiness that overcomes all darkness through suffering, trials, and forgiveness. The "happy ending" is not a cheap one, but a sure one, because it has already been attained through the victory of love in Christ. This book concludes with an interpretation of William Shakespeare's play *Measure for Measure*, which is set in Vienna; I had the honor of presenting this talk on the stage of the Vienna Burgtheater. I see it as a play that, in a manner unsurpassed in Shakespeare's work, treats the theme of forgiveness, without which no one in our chaotic world can succeed at having a happy life.

No work ends happily through individual achievement alone. Not even the various texts that are collected in this book. I ought to thank many people by name for conversations and exchanges with them, for their suggestions and help. Let me name just a few: Prof. Heinz Nußaumer, Prof. Erich Leitenberger, Dr. Michael Fritthum, Dr. Elisabeth Maier, Prof. Michael Waldstein, and my faithful coworker Josef Graisy, M.A. Finally I thank Dr. Brigitte Sinhuber of the publishing house Almathea Verlag for the patience with which she waited for the manuscript and Dr. Hubert Philipp Weber, who once again looked after it so well and proofread it so precisely. Anything unsuccessful about the book is to be charged to my account. The rest is gratitude, especially to the Lord, the Giver of all gifts.

Vienna, March 13, 2008,
the fourth anniversary of the death of Franz Cardinal König

† *Christoph Cardinal Schönborn*

I

HAPPINESS AND BEATITUDE

What Makes Life Happy

We were created to be happy

During my childhood and youth I heard many sermons, but I have no recollection whatsoever of their contents. I know they were often long, or at least they seemed long to me. I was not an attentive listener. Strangely enough, I remember one sentence, however, and only that one, but with complete clarity. It emerges clearly from the wide torrent of oblivion like a single star. It was a sermon of the pastor who was in charge of our parish during my adolescence. Beaming with love, kindness, humor, and intimate union with the Lord: although he died young and suddenly in 1966, that is how I and many others still remember him. At that time priests still preached from the pulpit, and I recall the feeling of benevolence that streamed down from that pulpit. What he was preaching about I have forgotten, just like the sermons of his predecessors, except for the one simple sentence: "We were created to be happy."

Perhaps I took note of this one solitary sentence because for me at the time, as a fifteen- or sixteen-year-old, it particularly suited my own search, or maybe also because our pastor himself radiated the truth of this sentence so credibly. (But what do we know exactly about the enigmatic ways of our memory?)

August 27, 2003, talk given at the Meeting of the People, Rimini (Italy).

"We were created to be happy." Hopefully you will take note of this one sentence at least. And even if you should forget it, along with everything else I am going to say, there is no reason to be concerned, because you will certainly not forget the matter. It is inscribed in the heart of every person as something self-evident, at least inasmuch as all philosophers agree that every person longs for happiness and strives for it. It is also obvious to common sense. Nobody wants to be unhappy or strives for unhappiness as such; at most someone is willing to put up with a certain amount of unhappiness for the sake of a greater happiness, or one makes the best of unhappiness because there are no more prospects of happiness in sight. But surely no one wishes for unhappiness as such. Yet the sentence in the pastor's sermon at my parish back home expresses more than the self-evident truth that all men want to be or to become happy. It means that this longing for happiness was given to us by the Creator; it does not deceive us; it is not a veil of illusion. It represents the destination intended for us by the Creator.

I remember precisely the strong interior feeling, the joyful surprise and consent, that this sentence evoked in me: Becoming happy, being happy, is not something forbidden; it is God's most characteristic will for us, his creatures. I am destined for happiness, and happiness for me; it awaits me, and I may joyfully expect it. If it comes to pass, I am allowed to accept it.

A happy man

When I try today, many years later, to explain why this saying moved me so much then that I have kept it in mind, I see two main reasons.

From the time when I was eleven years old I was already wondering whether I should become a priest. At the age of eleven, I was more certain than at the age of fifteen or sixteen. I had already experienced much unhappiness in my family. Was I supposed to or did I have to become a priest? Was I not allowed to live a "normal" life with a marriage and a family? On the other hand, I was attracted again and again to the priestly vocation. In the midst of this search, I took to heart the saying about being happy, and it had a liberating effect on me. Whatever my vocation, my path of life would be, God wanted to make me happy; it was for this that he created me.

A second, no less important element that made this saying so impressive and unforgettable for me was the fact that the man who pronounced it seemed happy to me. I have seldom met a human being who radiated so strongly from within the truth of this saying, the only one from all his sermons that I noticed: *a happy man*. On his lips this saying was convincing, because he himself witnessed to it with his whole life, indeed, with his whole being.

But what was it that convinced me that this priest was a happy man? What was it that moved everyone in our village to tears, even the old farmers, when he suddenly died and the parochial vicar read aloud his last will and testament? Was it his sense of humor? But that was only a sign of a deep "attunement" of his nature that is best described with the word "happy". Our pastor had often been sick; he had a great love for the sick, to whom he used to speak every week in a very popular radio program to which many healthy people also listened. Obviously sickness and suffering had been unable to take his cheerfulness away from him. His kindness and generosity were infectious, although sometimes they could give offense. Late in the evening the villagers could see a light burning in the church next to the tabernacle. His kneeler was the source of his inner strength.

When I was sixteen years old, he invited me to come along on a parish pilgrimage to Assisi, Rome, and Loreto.

The highlight, however, was a visit to Padre Pio (d. 1968). Although as a teenager at that time, I was reluctant to go along to see the famous priest with the stigmata, the Mass that he celebrated and the brief encounter with him afterward made an unforgettable impression on me. What was it? Who was that man from whom such power went out? Was he happy? Is "happiness" the right category with which to describe what he radiated and the reason people came in droves? Was his stigmatization, which lasted exactly fifty years, not a unique misfortune? Be that as it may, he certainly made many people happy, took away the burden of their sins through confession, and moved them to repentance. Through his great hospital he alleviated the sufferings of many sick people. It is certain that many came to him unhappy and burdened and went away relieved and happy again. And certainly we can describe Saint Pio of Pietrelcina as someone who suffered much, but not as an unhappy man.

"We were created to be happy." But what it means to be happy cannot be determined in the first place theoretically; to define that we need, more than anything else, experience, in a twofold sense: what I myself perceive and what I observe in others; my own personal awareness of happiness and my appreciation of other people's situation as "happy".

If it is true that the Christian way of life is considered to be an incomparable, outstanding path to happiness, then that must prove to be accurate in this twofold sense: it must be possible to experience it personally as a happy life and, at the same time, to see it as a happy life for others.

Now we all know that "happiness" is a deceptive thing. There are so many forms of apparent happiness, so many promises of happiness that do not last. I do not need to discuss them all in detail here; they are part of the classical repertoire of the moral sermons of philosophers, men of letters, and theologians. Money, fame, success, sex, and so on—all these can be fun, satisfying, pleasant, comforting. But they do not quite guarantee that one will be happy.

But it was self-evident to all of us back home that my pastor could be described as a happy man. About this there was something like an unmistakable certainty. Here it was clearly visible and perceptible: With this sort of being happy there is no danger of deception, no false appearance, no fleeting illusion. This happy existence attracted me. It was surely not unimportant for my decision to become a priest.

Happiness, small and great

Let us try to trace the paths of happiness in simple steps. I see two stages along this way. I call them simply *the small happiness* and *the great happiness*. I am convinced that the two are closely interdependent. There is a great temptation to underestimate the small happiness as something philistine, unspiritual, unheroic. Yet the small happiness is the preparatory school for the great happiness; it gives us a certain premonition, a foretaste of the latter.

By small happiness, I mean those joys in life that bring a little brightness into our all-too-often dreary routine: a good meal, a refreshing sleep, a cold glass of beer on a hot summer day, a game of cards on Sunday. Someone who cannot enjoy such little pleasures will also miss the great happiness.

The biblical skeptic Qoheleth invites his readers, in a world in which "all is vanity", *omnia vanitas* (Eccles 1:2), at least not to renounce the bit of happiness that often is to be had only in small portions:

> Go, eat your bread with enjoyment, and drink your wine with a merry heart; for God has already approved what you do.

Let your garments be always white; let not oil be lacking on your head.

Enjoy life with the wife whom you love, all the days of your vain life which he has given you under the sun. (Eccles 9:7–9)

Ideologues of all stripes have always despised the "small happiness" and instead have promised an allegedly "great happiness". The '68 generation [sixties protesters] disdained the joys of the small happiness as being petit bourgeois. Yet there is something profoundly inhumane in that disdain. People ridiculed—and still do ridicule—the "pursuite of happyness" that is anchored in the American Constitution, while forgetting that it is a preeminent duty of the State to ensure those basic conditions which provide enough space in people's lives for the small happiness. To achieve the great happiness is not the State's task, as the ideologies of the twentieth century, especially Marxism, set out to do. Much is accomplished already if societal relations are ordered in such a way that as many people as possible can lead a halfway happy life. To serve the *eu-zèn*, the "good life", is the noblest task of politics; it should not try to create a paradise on earth, for experience has shown that that leads to the gulags. According to the classic view of Aristotle, it should promote the good life by enabling people to enjoy a certain degree of wellbeing. One can criticize the American empire on several counts, but one thing is obvious: people from all over the world still seek that way of life, because they expect more happiness from it than from the living conditions in which they have to live in their native lands. And is being an "economic refugee" something bad, if one is looking for better living conditions? The Italians who emigrated to the United States or to Argentina "tried their luck" there, just like the Poles who went to the United States or to the industrial district in the Ruhr Valley (Germany) looking for jobs.

Morality and happiness

The *Catechism of the Catholic Church* quotes a statement by Pope Pius XII from an address dated June 1, 1941, that we cannot ponder enough. The Pope points out that there are deplorable societal conditions, inequities, unjust structures in the State and in social life that "make Christian conduct in keeping with the commandments of the divine Law-giver difficult and almost impossible" (CCC 1887).

In such situations it is often extremely difficult to prac-tice the simple virtues of honesty, truthfulness, decency, and integrity. In countries where corruption has seeped into all areas of life, it requires more than "normal virtue" to escape the undertow of corruption. Often then it is the quiet, hid-den saints who resist the pressure of the general depravity. Faced with the evil of a corrupt State, in a society devoured by corruption, even a "normal measure" of virtue requires heroism. In such circumstances the rug is pulled out from under the "happy life".

"Ethical relations" in dealings among the peoples of the world, in the life of a country, in the public climate of a soci-ety, are not just a luxury that we could do without; they are the prerequisite if people are to lead a halfway happy life.

The fact that Pope John Paul (d. 2005) so decisively objected to the war in Iraq was rooted in this certainty: only on the firm foundation of a legal order can a policy of peace be constructed. That is true in international law as well as in individual countries.

This No to the war in Iraq sprang, not from a naïve pacifism, but rather from a concern about observing inter-national law and also from a deep conviction that war is a

defeat of humanity. In this specific case, the Pope's clear
No also sounded the extremely important trumpet signal-
ing that the conflict is not a religious war between Christianity and Islam.

The Holy Father fought tirelessly to defend human life.
How can there be peace, one of the prerequisites for happiness, if the right to life of the weakest among us, the
unborn, is not protected?

The Pope was not only the defender of the special interests of the Catholic Church, but also the indefatigable *defen-
sor civitatis*, the defender of a just citizenry. He championed
human rights, the family, the unborn, social justice, and
peace in one great effort to make it possible for the individual and for communities to lead a "happy life".

The common good

The societal prerequisite for successfully bringing about a
(relatively) happy life is called in classical Christian social
doctrine *the common good* (*bonum commune*). I consider it
extremely urgent that the concept and the cause of the common good be clearly recognized and acknowledged once
again as the paramount task of politics.

The Second Vatican Council defines the common good
in *Gaudium et spes* as "the sum total of social conditions
which allow people, either as groups or as individuals, to
reach their fulfillment more fully and more easily" (*Gaudium et spes*, no. 26; CCC 1906).

Without concern for the common good, there is no room
for a happy life. Caring about the common good, however,
demands that three essential elements be safeguarded: respect
for the individual, social welfare, along with peace and security.

Without respect for the individual and his fundamental
rights, especially his civil rights and liberty, there can be no

social welfare, that is, those societal conditions which are the prerequisite for a humane, decent life: food, clothing, shelter, work, education, training, information, health care, the good of families, and so on. All this presupposes in turn that there is a lasting peace, "that is, the stability and security of a just order" (CCC 1909).

A State, a country, a community in which all these pre-conditions for the common good are fulfilled in a halfway decent manner is to be considered fortunate, or happy. No earthly community will ever fulfill these conditions perfectly, just as there will never be any perfect happiness on earth. But there is a fundamental difference between having to live under despotic rule, a dictatorship, and living in a free country. There is a tremendous difference between living in social and economic misery and living in a country that is prospering economically. Happiness and unhappiness are never absolute on this earth, yet there are situations of great unhappiness or rewarding happiness. It is possible for anyone with common sense to distinguish between them.

Who is remembered by the peoples of the world as a good leader? Not Napoleon, with his endless wars, but rather those who made it possible for their people to experience good times or at least made positive contributions to that end. Disqualified as good leaders, however, are also those who made good times possible in the short term, but at a cost that future generations had to pay dearly.

What judgment will future generations pass on our era, in view of the tremendous mountains of debt that we have piled up and that will weigh heavily on the generations to come? How will they judge our reckless and wasteful consumption of resources? Or the social inequities that cry out to heaven? Will their reproach not be: "You consumers had your affluence and your earthly happiness and left the bill for us to pay"? But are those not merely pulpit platitudes? Does not the reality look quite different?

Success is what counts, not the common good! Whoever has the power (or the media coverage) is king. Anyone who can bend the law to his own purposes should be right. What counts is not the old values of decency, virtue, or service; instead, whatever makes money and sells well in the media market wins applause and acclaim. It is becoming fashionable to set oneself above decency, authority, the law, and even to boast about it. Success confers authority; it does not matter whether it is based on righteousness or unrighteousness. This recalls Socrates' debates with the Sophists, which were foundational for Europe, and Jesus' words about the discernment of spirits: "You cannot serve two masters, God and mammon" (cf. Mt 6:24).

Wherever the philosophy of "might makes right" prevails, the life of the weaker ones is quickly deprived of that protective societal framework which makes a halfway decent, good, happy life possible.

Socrates made a decision in favor of righteousness, truth, and goodness and was ready to commit his life to it, indeed, to give up his life for it. Europe at its best has been supported again and again by the conviction that Socrates was the happier man, that his life stands as an example of a successful life, whereas the happiness of the Sophists, who rate success as more important than what is true and good, ultimately cannot be a desirable purpose in life.

Happiness and blessedness

With that, however, we come to the central point: What I called the small happiness, which we often learn to appreciate only when it is lost due to war, injustice, corruption, misery, and slander—this "small happiness" of a life spent in peace and security is supplied by a flowing spring: by the great happiness.

I would like to explain what I mean by the great happiness by looking, not to Socrates, one of the Fathers of Europe, but rather to "the greatest saint of the modern era", as Pius XI called her, to the Little Flower, Thérèse of Lisieux (d. 1897).

The words "bonheur", "heureux", "heureuse" [happiness, happy] appear quite often in her vocabulary. These are key words. It is no accident that we find talk about happiness in the key experience of the fourteen-year-old girl, in the "grace de Noël" (grace of Christmas) which was a decisive turning point in her life and marked the beginning of her "course de géant" [giant's course]. The sickly, hypersensitive Thérèse is once again near tears, but in an instant she experiences "the grace of my complete conversion". This was sparked by what was basically a small act of overcoming her sensitivity so as not to disappoint others, especially her father: "I felt *charity* enter into my soul, and the need to forget myself and to please others; since then I've been happy!" [1]

Thérèse—a happy person! What kind of happiness? What was its source? And how did it become the source of happiness for many? Socrates came near to this source. It was first opened on Golgotha. It flows from the pierced side of the Crucified One, who came in order to make the great happiness known and to invite people to share in it.

My pastor's life spoke to me about this happiness; I perceived this happiness in a frightening, deeply moving way in Padre Pio. And only when I began to taste this great happiness did the small happiness start to taste good as well.

---

[1] Thérèse of Lisieux, *Story of a Soul: The Autobiography of St. Thérèse of Lisieux*, trans. John Clarke, O.C.D., 2nd ed. (Washington, D.C.: ICS Publications, 1976), 99.

The promise of this great happiness stands at the beginning of Jesus' preaching, when eight times on the mountain in Galilee he describes certain people as especially happy, as "blessed" (Mt 5:3–12).

"The Beatitudes reveal the goal of human existence, the ultimate end of human acts: God calls us to his own beatitude", says the *Catechism of the Catholic Church* (CCC 1719). What kind of happiness does Jesus promise in the Beatitudes? At first glance what Jesus mentions here does not correspond to conventional notions of happiness. One might reasonably see why God promises happiness to the peacemakers, the meek, the pure of heart, and those who hunger for justice. But it is difficult to understand why the poor, the sorrowing, indeed, those who are persecuted in all sorts of ways should be happy. Where, then, do we find the key to the "great happiness"? In the very same place where we find the key to the "small happiness". Where, then?

Folk wisdom in all parts of the world notes that happiness cannot be made but rather "happens" to a person. Happiness in the secular sense is notoriously moody and changeable. "O fortuna, velut luna" (O fortune, like the moon), we read in the *Carmina Burana*. The man who won the sixty-six-million-Euro jackpot did not earn it. Everyone says that he was "lucky"—as long as he is not doomed by the money instead. "Good fortune", the small happiness that is something quite different from luck at the lottery, can be attained only with the attitude of receptivity, of selflessness. It has something to do with grace, favor, gift. At the same time it has its roots in devotion to a purpose, in harnessing and directing one's strength to complete a task or to do a work.

A child at play is completely given over to the activity of the game, and at the same time the game shows precisely the character of gift, of something not simply available. The happiness of child's play is at the same time gratuitousness and recollected self-giving.

The mountain climber finds his happiness by reaching the summit—which is at the same time the result of his single-minded devotion to the goal for which he is striving and the overwhelming gift that crowns and surpasses all his efforts.

Both elements obviously are part of happiness, both the small and the great: self-giving and gift, striving for a goal and grateful receptivity. The key to happiness lies precisely in this tension. If striving, accomplishment, and efforts of all sorts are motivated by a longing for one's own glory or mere self-realization, they will not make a person happy. If they are done out of a devotion to a purpose, out of an interest that is forgetful of self, they can lead to moments of great joy and intense happiness, which are then experienced as pure gift. Viewed philosophically, this key could help to overcome the Kantian dilemma between fulfillment of duty and striving for happiness.

Happiness and self-giving

Thérèse has shown us the path. For her the key to happiness was "to forget myself so as to please others" (m'oublier pour faire plaisir). The Second Vatican Council formulated it in a similar way in a passage that was one of those most often cited during the pontificate of John Paul II: "Man can fully discover his true self only in a sincere giving of himself (per sincerum sui ipsius donum)" (*Gaudium et spes*, no. 24). That is what it means to become happy. The Holy Father cited this central thesis of Christian anthropology numerous times and demonstrated how it applies to all areas of life. Most importantly, however, his whole life made the truth of this thesis visible. Although what he lived, endured, and suffered by no means corresponded to "worldly" notions of happiness, we certainly cannot describe him as an unhappy man. He showed the world what a happy life is. Surely he "fully discovered his true self" (cf. *Gaudium et spes*, no. 24).

The Second Vatican Council also shows why self-giving is the source of "fully discovering oneself" and, thus, of happiness. Jesus' prayer to his Father, the Council says, "that they may all be one . . . , even as we are one" (Jn 17:21f.) suggests a certain similarity between the union of the Divine Persons and the union of men, of the children of God, in truth and love (cf. *Gaudium et spes*, no. 24). Nowhere is this similarity more clearly evident than in man's vocation to the happiness that is God himself and that consists in nothing other than the complete self-giving of the Divine Persons to one another in the mystery of the Love that is God.

The *Catechism of the Catholic Church* begins with the words: "God [is] infinitely perfect and blessed in himself" (CCC 1). Man's great happiness, from which his small happiness also flows, is the "giving of himself" that constitutes God's being and to which God has called us, so that we, too, might have a share in his happiness. The *Catechism* goes on to say this: "[I]n a plan of sheer goodness [God] freely created man to make him share in his own blessed life" (CCC 1). Here we are again with the very same sentence of my pastor back home: "We were created to be happy." Now, though, it has become clear that the path to the happiness for which we were created leads by way of the "sincere giving of oneself" (cf. *Gaudium et spes*, no. 24).

That is why so many people, even without prompting, regard the saints as human beings in the full sense, whose lives were completely successful and happy. In them shines God's own beatitude. In them we see that a life of self-giving is a happy life. Hanna-Barbara Gerl-Falkovitz, the famous German philosopher, concludes her essay on happiness with a reference to the saying of Jesus that gives expression to the dialectic of happiness: "Wanting to gain the whole world means losing oneself; losing oneself for Christ's sake means gaining the whole world and oneself as well. Happiness, then, becomes conferred identity: being gathered into a center that is not one's own." [2]

Happiness and mercy

We could conclude with those words of the philosopher. I think, though, that at least two additional remarks are indispensable, so that our talk about happiness does not remain up in the air, so to speak.

1. In a very moving essay, Godfried Cardinal Danneels pointed out the necessary connection between happiness and forgiveness. On earth and most certainly in eternity there is no happiness unless there is first the gift of forgiveness.

How often the psalms celebrate the happiness of forgiveness. When relations between men are disrupted, when hatred, conflict, and enmity poison everything, then only true forgiveness can make the sources of happiness flow again. Anyone who has experienced it knows what a source of happiness forgiveness is. And this source, too, has its origins in God himself. "The love of God", says Cardinal Danneels, "is not content to *give*; it wants to *forgive*, too." [3] And above all it has to do with God's self-giving. It springs from the source of the greatest, most perfect self-giving, the Cross: "Father, forgive them: for they know not what they do" (Lk 23:34). All the saints knew that: The door to happiness

[2] "Glück ohne Verdienst? Das Doppelgesicht des Glücks", in H.-B. Gerl-Falkovitz, *Eros, Glück, Tod und andere Versuche im christlichen Denken* (Gräfelfing, 2001), 66–81.

[3] Godfried Cardinal Danneels, *Le Stress du bonheur* (Mechelen, 2002), 42.

opens only with the key of the Cross. That is why the First (Roman) Eucharistic Prayer speaks paradoxically about his "blessed Passion" (tam beata passio).

2. On August 17, 2002, Pope John Paul II consecrated the Shrine of Divine Mercy in Łagiewniki near Krakow. On that occasion he used extraordinarily forceful words that have a great, worldwide significance. They are the core of the Christian Good News. In the place where a nun, Saint Faustina (d. 1938), received revelations about the mercy of God—"Supreme attribute of Almighty God, You are the sweet hope for sinful man"[4]—the Holy Father said: "In God's mercy the world will find peace and man will find happiness!" Where else could we men, burdened with sins and plagued by injustices, misery, and conflicts, find "an inexhaustible source of hope" if not in the "incomprehensible and limitless divine mercy"?[5] In view of the mercy of Jesus, we become conscious of the whole depth and wickedness of sin, on the one hand, but at the same time of the assurance that all sins, even the most serious, are forgiven if we trust in the mercy of God.

At the conclusion of his homily in Łagiewniki, the Holy Father "consecrate[d] the world solemnly to the Divine Mercy" and expressed "the fervent wish that the message of God's merciful love ... might reach *all the people* in the world and fill their hearts with hope". His appeal, "*Be witnesses to mercy!*" is the concrete form in which the vocation to happiness should be proclaimed, especially today.

[4] Faustina Kowalska, *Tagebuch*, ed. Josef Stimpfle et al., 7th ed. (Hauteville, Switzerland, 2006), 951.

[5] Ibid.

Love and Friendship
in Thomas Aquinas

The one essential thing at the heart of every happy human and Christian life is friendship. It is of this I would like to speak. I have in my own life experienced that friendship is the most precious of all goods, and I am convinced that Saint Thomas Aquinas (d. 1274) made friendship the point on which his whole theological work turns, since he defined love, which no doubt is the quintessence of Christianity, as friendship. For many years these thoughts have occupied me. I consider the treatise on love in the *Secunda Secundae* (the second part of the second book) of the *Summa Theologiae* to be the key, so to speak, to the whole work. I think that all the major themes and concerns of Aquinas are gathered and brought into focus in this treatise. Of course it is impossible to expound the entire treatise in the short time allotted to this talk. Still, I would like to try at least to present some of the central ideas of "*quaestio 23*", which is devoted to the nature of love.

Is love friendship?

Saint Thomas begins his treatise on love immediately with the question of whether it is a kind of friendship. In keeping with his usual method, he begins first with objections to this

June 8, 2002, commencement address, Thomas Aquinas College, Santa Paula, California.

supposition. They are weighty, as they always are when Saint Thomas broaches an important theme. He deliberately tries to make the counterarguments especially strong, so as then to present his assertion in a way that is even more clear and well founded. This method does not disparage or belittle the opponent, but rather brings out his arguments in the strongest and most concise possible way, so as to underscore the seriousness of the struggle to attain the truth. Saint Thomas never needs to malign or make light of those who think differently, because he is convinced that the light of truth shines brightly enough to prevail on its own.

For Thomas it is self-evident that love is the center and quintessence of the Christian life; after all, the commandment of love of God and love of neighbor is considered the epitome of the Law and thus of the will of God. But that love is a sort of friendship is anything but self-evident. Can there be friendship between God and man, when living together with the friend is an essential element of friendship? We are supposed to love God. But having friendly relations with God is not simply a given that we can take for granted.

The second objection likewise considers friendship to be a narrower concept than the concept of love. Jesus commanded us to love our enemies. Therefore it is possible to love them, but one cannot cultivate friendship with one's enemies. The third objection, too, is along these lines: I may be able to love sinners with the love of God. Does that mean that I can also be friends with them?

The objections seem, therefore, to aim at proving that friendship is something more restricted than love. Love knows no limits; it extends to God and to all mankind. Friendship, in contrast, is possible only with one's equals and with those with whom we have ties of goodwill.

The argument supporting the thesis of Saint Thomas is taken from Jesus' farewell discourse at the Last Supper, when

our Lord says to the Twelve, "No longer do I call you servants ... but I have called you friends" (Jn 15:15). When I
was consecrated a bishop, I took this saying of Jesus as my
motto: *Vos autem dixi amicos.* The one and only reason why
our Lord calls his apostles friends is, according to Thomas,
his love. Therefore the sort of love that Jesus bestowed on
his disciples is proved to be friendship.

The argumentation that now follows in the main part of
the first article is for me one of the greatest and most beautiful passages in the whole theological *Summa.* In a few strokes
the Angelic Doctor not only sketches a doctrine about friendship but also sees the final purpose of all of God's salvific works
in the establishment of a friendship between God and man.
Let us examine somewhat the lines of the argument.

In an earlier article, Thomas had already asked the question of whether it is right and appropriate to divide love
(*amor*) into the love of friendship (*amor amicitiae*) and the
love of concupiscence or desire (*amor concupiscentiae*). For
love is treated by Thomas first under the aspect of passion
(*passio*), as the fundamental form of the passion of desire
(*concupiscibilis*). There (*quaestio* 26, *art.* 4 of the *Prima Secundae*)
he has already explained that the love that is friendship is
undoubtedly superior to the love that is desire. For desire is
concerned with something I would like to have for myself.
The love of friendship, however, is concerned with the good
I wish for the other person. Love, however, is realized more
fully when I want something good for another than when
I am concerned about my own good.

Establishing friendship

Now article 1 in question 23 also presupposes this framing
of the question. Thomas begins with the quotation from
the farewell discourse: "No longer do I call you servants ...

but ... friends" (Jn 15:15). But what sort of friendship is it that Jesus is talking about and that he grants to his disciples? "The Philosopher", that is, Aristotle, gives the cue here. Not every love, he says, has the quality of friendship. In order for love to become friendship, it must have the character of goodwill (*benevolentia*). As long as we want something only for our own sake, it is the love of concupiscence. If it is said that someone loves wine, it would be ridiculous to maintain that there is a friendship in that instance. The wine is loved, not for its own sake, but rather for the sake of the joy that it gives me. In this sense Thomas also excludes the possibility that there could be a friendship between a man and a horse. (He must not have read the *Narnia* books by C. S. Lewis; otherwise he would probably have spoken differently about the friendship between boys and horses.) The decisive element, however, is not just benevolence. Friendship exists only when there is *mutual* goodwill, for "only the friend is friend to the friend", as Aristotle says. There must be reciprocity, therefore, and this presupposes real communication between the friends. We all are familiar with the painful experience of friendships fading when they are not constantly nourished by mutual exchange, conversation, and encounters.

But can there be a real reciprocity between God and man? Is not the distance between God and man infinite and thus ultimately unbridgeable? It is the most profound conviction of the Christian faith that God really communicates something of himself to us and, furthermore, that he has given himself to us in his Son and in the Holy Spirit. God shares his life with us, and that is why there is a true mutual relation of communion. More precisely: that is why it is possible to establish a friendship on the basis of this gift of God's self-communication. If there is one expression that, in my opinion, summarizes the entire *Summa Theologiae*, it is *fundari amicitiam*. God wills "to establish a friendship" with his creature. The whole path of human and Christian life has its most profound meaning in this process of establishing friendship with God. And the whole ethics of interpersonal communication among men is summarized in this one expression: establishing friendship.

The prologue to the second book of the *Summa* is very important. There man's entire path is depicted from the perspective of the image and likeness of God. Man is created in God's likeness and is therefore called to realize this divine image by freely moving toward his destination. Continuing now in the vein of this prologue, we can now say more precisely that the entire meaning of human life consists in realizing the likeness of God in friendship with God. Thomas makes it clear that this establishment of a friendship also has a very specific place: fellowship and thus friendship with Jesus Christ. In him God has communicated himself completely to us men. That is why it is essential to establish friendship with God specifically as friendship with Jesus Christ, who came to make us his friends.

Let us look at the replies that Saint Thomas gives to the three objections:

Reply to objection 1. It is true that, at least in our bodily life, there is no immediate fellowship with God. It does exist, however, in the spiritual life. For even now our life is hidden with Christ in God, as the Apostle says (Col 3:3). Hence we already have now a real, albeit imperfect, fellowship with God that will be perfected in the beatific vision of God.

Reply to objection 2. Here Saint Thomas proves very beautifully the possibility of loving one's enemy. There can be no friendship with an enemy; that is possible only between friends. But the friends of my friends nevertheless become in a certain sense my friends also, even though they are not directly congenial to me. If friendship with God unites us, then on the basis of this friendship we also love those for whom God did not hesitate to send his Son, even though they are our enemies.

Reply to objection 3. The same is true also of love for sinners. Even though direct friendship with them does not seem appropriate, the love that God has for them (and for us too, since we ourselves are sinners) is reason enough to regard them with God's love and in this light to love them also with the love of friendship.

This first and fundamental article of the treatise on love has provided us with the decisive keyword: *fundari amicitiam*. Now it is a question of examining more closely how this friendship between God and us is to be obtained, how it can grow and fully develop.

Friendship with God

In the second article of question 23, the doctrine of love as friendship between God and man is once again deepened in a crucial way. The point of departure is the statement by Peter Lombard (d. 1160), the Master of the *Sentences*, that love is not something created but rather the Holy Spirit himself, who dwells in our soul. In other words, God himself is the love in us. On account of its greatness and pre-eminent importance, love cannot be something created; it must be immediately divine—indeed, God himself. At first reading, that sounds very pious and sublime. Thomas, however, makes it clear that this makes love, not greater, but fundamentally smaller. In what way?

If the Holy Spirit himself were the love in us, then it would not be an act or an attitude (*habitus*) of the man. For then loving would not be up to us; it would not depend on our will. We ourselves would not love, but God in us would be loving himself. Here we come across the central point in the anthropology of Saint Thomas, which has implications for all areas of human life. Love would not be love and could not be friendship if it were not also, on the part of man, a genuine, human act (that is, voluntary and rational). If we were moved "passively" to love, like a tool in the hand of a craftsman, then it would not be love, for, as the first article demonstrated, when love is friendship, then reciprocity is an essential feature of it.

But that is precisely what God enables us to do through the communication of himself, whereby he makes us capable of establishing a friendship with him. Thomas formulates it in his own language as follows: In order to be able to love God in friendship, we need a capability that surpasses our natural abilities and makes us "connatural" with God, so to speak, a capability that makes it possible for us really to love God and to be united to him in friendship.

The explanations of Saint Thomas in the second article are also a textbook example of his method, from which we can learn much. Only in the rarest cases do we find polemics in Thomas. He always tries to strengthen the arguments of those whose viewpoint he does not share. Since he is quite objectively concerned about the truth, he strives to emphasize the portion of truth found in other positions, however unlike his own. This becomes evident precisely in this article. As a young professor he wrote a commentary on the *Sentences* of Master Peter Lombard, which was then the usual university textbook. Hence he respectfully presents the Master's postulate, too. Just as respectful is the way in which he corrects that position: "If we consider the matter aright, this (that is, the Master's position) would be, *on the contrary*, detrimental to charity [love]." Now the Master was part of the Augustinian tradition, and in reference to Augustine (d. 430), Thomas carefully notes that this manner of speaking (namely, identifying the love in man with God himself) was customary among the Platonic philosophers and that Augustine had been steeped (*imbutus*) in Platonic teachings. This led to many errors, which Thomas carefully but clearly corrects here.

Conclusions

We do not show any particular loyalty to Saint Thomas by defending his opinions as polemically as possible against all other possible viewpoints. We imitate his thought and his virtues to the extent that our search for truth motivates us to consult it wherever we find traces of it. Saint Thomas could never have integrated Aristotle so intensively had he not been supported by the conviction that Christ, the Eternal Word, is the Truth that enlightens every man. Wherever a ray of the light of truth can be found, it is important to inquire, to listen, so as to greet with joy the truth that is manifesting itself. Part of this, of course, is a constant willingness to expose and refute errors for the sake of truth. Both of these, however, greeting the truth and refuting error, require that one be well prepared to converse. Saint Thomas incomparably conducted a dialogue with all the masters of the past and the present. There is probably no better or more reliable guide to a Christian culture of dialogue than Saint Thomas.

Quaestio 23 indicates, so to speak, the anthropological and theological foundation on which this truly Christian and humanistic attitude of Saint Thomas is based: his image of God and man. There can be friendship only when there is genuine reciprocity in freedom: *mutuus amor, mutua inhaesio*, a real togetherness with and in each other.

The great thing about Saint Thomas' image of God is that he sees God, not only as the First Cause of everything, but also as being so powerful and great that he has given his creatures the power to be causes themselves, the ability to work on their own and not just passively to be moved by the supreme principle, by the First Cause.

Especially today it would be very timely and important to study carefully Saint Thomas' discussion with Islamic philosophy, especially that of Averroes. Thomas fought with all the power of his mind against Averroes' teaching that God alone is the cause of all. God is not exalted by diminishing his creatures. His true greatness is manifested, not in the complete powerlessness of creatures, but rather in their empowerment to be able to work on their own as causes.

The consequence of this view is the whole breadth of the Catholic understanding of secondary causes, of the relative autonomy of secular areas of activity. In my opinion it could be demonstrated that the scientific culture of countries with a Christian character has to do with this view of the independent efficacy of creatures. One would have to show, furthermore, how the Western understanding of participation and democracy developed out of this view. The consequences of Christian humanism become particularly evident in the area of human dignity and human rights.

Of course one would also have to discuss the dangers inherent in this humanism, which come to light when the dependence of the secondary causes on the First Cause is denied, when the autonomy of the world and of man forgets that it is creaturely and arrogates to itself an independence that it does not in fact possess.

There is probably no better place to study this paradox and to take it to heart than the treatise of Saint Thomas on love as friendship: the paradox of the freedom granted to man by God, of the reciprocity between the Eternal One and us that is made possible by God, of the real friendship between him, the Infinite One, and us, his mortal creatures.

II

GOD

"Holy is his name"

Meditation on the Name of God

In the *Tao-tê ching*, the holy book of Taoism, it says: "The name that can be named is not the eternal name" (chap. 1); and farther on (chap. 14): "A continuous thread beyond description ... thus you grasp the continuity of the way [Tao]." Everything that has the character of a "thing" can be named: "Names arose when differentiation commenced" (chap. 32). The Tao is unutterable; it is not even God in the biblical sense. It has no name because no name can exhaustively designate it.[1]

Should not reverence for the unutterable mystery of the Absolute prevent us from trying to confine it in a specific name? Is not the attempt to give God a name a temptation we must resist in view of God's greatness?

Does not the revelation of the Divine Name in the burning bush signify, rather, the refusal to give a name? The Jewish philosopher Philo of Alexandria (d. A.D. 40) interpreted this extremely important passage about the revelation of the Divine Name to Moses (Ex 3:13–15) in this

February 6, 2004, Ave Maria Lectures for Christ and the Religions, Aquinas Center in Naples, Florida. This lecture was first given in the Lateran Basilica on January 26, 1999.

[1] W. Eichhorn, "Der 'Name Gottes' in den religiösen Strömungen des alten China", in *Der Name Gottes*, ed. H. von Stietencron, 73f. (Düsseldorf, 1975).

way: "Now if they (the Israelites) ask me (Moses), what is the name of him who is sending me, but I myself cannot name him, then will I not appear to be a deceiver?" God answered (as Philo interprets the passage): "First tell them that I am the One-who-is (Greek: *ego eimi ho on*), so that when they have understood the difference between being and non-being, they might also learn that for Me, to whom alone being belongs, there is no proper name at all." [2] No name can name God, and if a name could, then it would not be naming God, the Unutterable.

Is this not the appropriate attitude toward the infinite, ineffable mystery of God? The Anaphora of Saint John Chrysostom (d. 407), that is, the Eucharistic Prayer of the Byzantine Liturgy, begins with the words: ". . . for you are God—ineffable, inconceivable, invisible, incomprehensible, always existing and ever the same."

And yet the astounding fact remains that the Old Testament understands the revelation of God to be "precisely the revelation of his name" and that this is maintained without a doubt well into the late New Testament era: "I have manifested your name to the men whom you gave me out of the world", as Jesus prays in the high priestly prayer (Jn 17:6). [3]

God has a name. The unutterable, infinitely mysterious One, the Eternal One reveals himself, names his name, and in this name, which belongs to him alone, he himself becomes present, unites himself to the people to whom he reveals his name and who will one day be his people—the people who bear his name and through whom he desires to proclaim his name to all peoples. To this people of his he also will send the One who will definitively reveal his name:

[2] Philo of Alexandria, *Vita Mosis* I, 74f.
[3] Cf. H. Gese, "Der Name Gottes im Alten Testament", in Stietencron, *Name Gottes*, 76.

Jesus, the Christ, the Son of the Living God (Mt 16:16). About him Peter, the Apostle, will profess that "there is no other name under heaven given among men by which we must be saved" (Acts 4:12; cf. CCC 432).

The name of God, revealed in the burning bush and on Sinai, is unique. Of all the names that are given to the Unutterable One yet cannot name him, this one name is really God's own name. To this day that is Israel's creed: "Hear, O Israel, YHWH [the LORD] is our God, the one (and only) YHWH" (Deut 6:4). And this one name has come still closer to us: he dwells not only in Israel; he dwells "bodily" (Col 2:9) in Jesus of Nazareth, to whom God gave "the name which is above every name" (Phil 2:9), "[so] that at the name of Jesus every knee should bow, in heaven and on earth and under the earth" (Phil 2:10). God has a name, God has a face, we can call him by name, and we are privileged to see his face: *Jesus.*

At this point in our meditation we need to illuminate several aspects of this revelation of the name. Let us begin by inquiring again more precisely into the meaning of the revelation of the name in the burning bush. That will lead to the question of how to "cope" with this scandal, that God reveals himself specifically, "by name", and does so, moreover, to a small, insignificant, semi-nomadic people in the Near East. We will then go on to ask what significance that has for the presence of God in the peoples and religions that name and revere God with many names. This will become an even more crucial question when we meditate on the name of Jesus, in whom God makes his mystery dwell in its entirety and reveals it definitively. We need to address the uniqueness of Jesus Christ. We conclude our meditation with the question about hallowing the name, for which our Lord has taught us to pray in the Our Father.

The revelation of the name in the burning bush

The Bible is acquainted with many names of God, but none has the importance that the revelation of the name of God in the burning bush has. There God revealed to Moses his name: "I AM WHO I AM" (Ex 3:14). "This is my name for ever, and thus I am to be remembered throughout all generations" (Ex 3:15).

How are we supposed to grasp in a few words the mystery of this name, which many generations of Jews and Christians have pondered and discussed? Faced with such a task, we would have to despair and lose heart. The scholars do not even know what this *ähjä 'ᵃ sär 'ähjä* really means: "I am who I am", "I prove to be whom I shall prove to be", "I am whom I shall prove to be"—to name just a few translations.

I would like to try, cautiously, an approach that to me seems helpful: What happens in the revelation of God's name to Moses, who while tending sheep not far from Mount Horeb sees a thornbush burning but not consumed? When Moses draws near this "great sight" (Ex 3:3), God calls to him out of the burning bush, "I am the God of your father, the God of Abraham, the God of Isaac, and the God of Jacob" (Ex 3:6). What takes place here is an initiative that proceeds from God. God's revelation is not "neutral information" but rather a deed. He is the God who has already decided the destiny of the patriarchs. Even though he did not yet reveal his name to Abraham, he nevertheless allowed himself to be known to him by calling to Abraham, "go from your country" (Gen 12:1).

Now, too, in the burning bush, God gives a command: "I have seen the affliction of my people who are in Egypt.... I know their sufferings, and I have come down to deliver them out of the hand of the Egyptians.... Come, I will send you ... that you may bring forth my people, the sons of Israel, out of Egypt ... I will be with you" (Ex 3:7–8, 10, 12).

"If ... they ask me, 'What is his name?' what shall I say to them?" Then God says to Moses, "I AM WHO I AM" (Ex 3:13–14). In revealing his name, God does something at the same time. He utters a promise and binds himself by his promise: "I will be with you." God's name is a promise. To a questioning, doubting Moses, God surrenders his name, so that he might trust him and respond wholeheartedly to his call: "Who am I that I should ... bring the sons of Israel out of Egypt?" (Ex 3:11). Moses is not to look at his own weakness but, rather, trust in the One who calls and sends him. His name is to give confidence to Moses and the people. In revealing it, he promises that he will be the One who he is.

What happens when we promise something? It is characteristic of man that he can make promises. An animal cannot. We can take responsibility today for what we will do in the future: "I promise you that on an appointed day I will give a lecture." What happens when we promise something? "To promise means not only that I am now willing to do or not to do something specific in the future, but also that I grant to someone else the title to rely on the fact that I will be willing later on also to keep this promise, that is, to be the same person that I am now, although I certainly will no longer be identical."[4]

Our entire human coexistence is based on promising and trusting. It is one of the foundations of all human relations that I—despite all vicissitudes, all changes—remain the same person. This is the basis for marriage and friendship, but

[4] Robert Spaemann, "Person und Versprechen", in *Kontinuität der Person: Zum Versprechen und Vertrauen*, ed. R. Schenk, 4, Reihe Collegium Philosophicum 2 (Stuttgart and Bad Cannstatt, 1998).

also for commercial, economic, and legal relations. Nothing disrupts human coexistence more than breaking a promise, unfaithfulness toward a person to whom we have pledged something. It causes trust to falter; indeed, it can even destroy it. A trustworthy business partner is one on whom you can rely, who abides by contracts. Trust is the basis of good business relations. The reason why marriage is so endangered today is that the mutual promise is no longer capable of supporting the weight that it should. When two people promise each other fidelity, they anticipate the future: What we promise each other today will still be valid in ten, in fifteen, in fifty years. The other person should be able to have confidence that that will be so, that the mutual promise stands firm and will last. That is the basis of trust. In promising, we make a pledge to one another: You can trust me: even then I will still be the one that I promise you today to be.

With a lecture that I promise to give, the matter is relatively simple. But a wedding vow, a priestly vow of fidelity, which a young person makes for a lifetime, or religious vows to live constantly and perpetually by the three evangelical counsels—obedience, poverty, and chastity—promises like that are a bold venture. For "promises bind the person who made them, but not in such a way that they determine him in the future like a law of nature does. It lies within our freedom not to keep the promise. And nevertheless the promise is binding. With it the person lifts himself as a free agent out of the deterministic stream of time. I might indeed be of a different mind later than I am now, when I make the promise." [5] It is a painful experience that we often change our minds and do not keep our promises. But on the other hand, that is precisely the greatness of the

[5] Ibid., 5–6.

human person, that he can lift himself above the change-ability of time and make himself independent of it: "I say now what I will do and therefore will want to do at a later point in time, even if the only reason is because I said so now." [6] "Pacta sunt servanda": Contracts are to be observed, says an ancient Roman principle of law, thus expressing a moral demand that is valid in all ages.

It is part of the nature and dignity of the human person that he has "contract capability" and thus can make and keep promises. However it is also a primordial human experience that the human heart wavers, a promise is not kept, and trust is disappointed.

In Moses' questioning and hesitation to respond whole-heartedly to God's call, to trust his name, we can sense all the human mistrust that we all know only too well. How will it be made manifest that God really is the "I am who am"? It will be manifested by the fact that he is as his name indicates: "I prove to be who I will prove to be." God proves that his name expresses his nature and that Moses, and all of us subsequently, can trust him and respond wholeheart-edly to his call. Through the "signs and wonders" that he works in order to liberate Israel from Egypt, God proves his name, he "hallows" it. The greatest of all the signs and wonders is the Exodus itself, the departure from Egypt. God leads his people "with a mighty hand and an outstretched arm". To this day the remembrance of this event, cel-ebrated and made present every year in the Passover, is for our Jewish "elder brethren" the proof par excellence that God is he who reveals his name to us: he is the "I am here" for his people. If God has proved to be the One who has remained faithful to his promise to the patriarchs, then he will prove faithful today also and in the future. That is why

[6] Ibid., 6.

it is so important for Israel to bear in mind all of God's deeds: "Forget not all his benefits!"

The proof of forgiveness

Among all the deeds of God remembered by Israel, there is none so astonishing as his forgiveness. God stands by his promise, even when his people are unfaithful. Besides the revelation of the name in the burning bush, another great revelation is granted to Moses: the one on Mount Sinai after the people fall into sin with the golden calf (Ex 32–34). Despite all the proofs that he is God, that his name is true, the people fall away from him, demand a visible, tangible god, and make for themselves a golden calf: "These are your gods, O Israel, who brought you up out of the land of Egypt!" (Ex 32:4). For Israel, this falling away from the living God serves as the prototype of its sins: infidelity toward him who proves to be faithful. A second time now God reveals his name, this time in order to liberate his people, not from external slavery in Egypt, but rather from a much more momentous captivity, from sin. God appears to Moses once again on Mount Sinai, and in revealing his name once more, he again does what this name says: he forgives the guilt of his people. The Lord passes before Moses and cries, "The LORD, the LORD, a God merciful and gracious, slow to anger, and abounding in steadfast love and faithfulness" (Ex 34:6). What an astonishing utterance: God himself proclaims his name! And by revealing himself as the merciful and gracious One, he forgives his people their sins and reestablishes the covenant himself. Never does God reveal his name, that is, his inmost being, so profoundly as when he manifests himself as being "rich in mercy" (Eph 2:4). His name, "I am who I am here", proves to be a deed and a promise precisely in the forgiveness of sin, that is, of our infidelity, of our unkept promises.

Hence it is no accident that in Israel the holy name of God is pronounced only once a year, by the high priest, in the Holy of Holies in the Temple: on *Yom Kippur*, the great Day of Atonement. God's name thus becomes the place of forgiveness. Israel calls on God's name, not only so as to be rescued from external distress, but even more importantly for the sake of salvation from sin.

Countless times the name of God is invoked in Israel so as to move God in his inmost being, his *rachamim* (literally, "bowels"), to manifest that he is who he is: the God of mercy, "slow to anger and abounding in steadfast love" (Ex 34:6). Of the many examples let this one suffice:

> Though our iniquities testify against us,
>> act, O LORD, for your name's sake;
> for our backslidings are many,
>> we have sinned against you.
> O you hope of Israel,
>> its savior in time of trouble,
> why should you be like a stranger in the land,
>> like a wayfarer who turns aside to linger for a night?
> … Yet you, O LORD, are in the midst of us,
>> And we are called by your name;
>> leave us not. (Jer 14:7–9)

The theme that God's name is forgiveness runs like a leitmotiv through the Psalms and the prophets: "For your name's sake, O LORD, pardon my guilt, for it is great" (Ps 25:11).

> Let your compassion come speedily to meet us,
>> for we are brought very low.
> Help us, O God of our salvation,
>> for the glory of your name;
> deliver us, and forgive our sins,
>> for your name's sake! (Ps 79:8–9)

On its journey with God, Israel recognized ever more clearly that earthly liberation may perhaps be accomplished even by human power, but from the power of sin only One can save, the One whose name brings salvation: "You, O LORD are our Father, our Redeemer from of old is your name" (Is 63:16).

What God's most proper name is and promises, he himself will bring about by revealing his name once again "when the time had fully come" (Gal 4:4). He will have it "take up residence" in our midst: in Jesus Christ. "She will bear a son, and you shall call his name Jesus, for he will save his people from their sins" (Mt 1:21).

His name means "God saves." In Jesus, the most proper name of God "became flesh and dwelt among us" (Jn 1:14). He is the promised Emmanuel, "which means, God with us" (Mt 1:23). Jesus is the perfect expression of God's name. What God revealed to Moses in the burning bush and on Sinai, the mystery of his name, has become bodily present in Jesus Christ: "For in him the whole fulness of deity dwells bodily" (Col 2:9). In him God fulfills the promise inherent in his name: the deliverance and redemption that all men need, without exception. That is why we believe and profess that salvation is in him and in no other: "For there is no other name under heaven given among men by which we must be saved" (Acts 4:12).

And so we worship Jesus Christ: "For you alone are the Holy One, you alone are the Lord, you alone are the Most High, Jesus Christ, with the Holy Spirit, in the glory of God the Father", as it says in the Gloria.

Three consequences

What has been sketched here briefly and summarily has far-reaching consequences. We should mention three of them in conclusion.

1. If God's name is unique, and if God has revealed his mystery, himself, and thus "in a way has handed himself over" (cf. CCC 203), then the recipient of his revelation is also unique: "the people of Israel who are near to him" (Ps 148:14). "He has not dealt thus with any other nation; they do not know his ordinances" (Ps 147:20).

2. God is not a nameless power, "not an anonymous force" (CCC 203), but has a name; therefore the people he has chosen so as to proclaim his name to it alone has become the bearer of his name forever: Israel.

One of the most burning questions for theology and the Church today concerns the meaning and significance for salvation of the many religions in the world. Are not all religions pathways leading to God? Do not the many ways to God correspond to the many names of the Unutterable? Is not the "particularism" of a unique revelation to a single recipient a sign of terrible intolerance? Has not the one, infinitely mysterious God revealed himself in many different ways, so that every religion captures only one ray of his light but never all of it? Does not the "claim to absoluteness" of one revelation necessarily lead to all the evils of religious wars, fundamentalism, and so on?

These questions occupy many theologians today, especially in Asia, yet they are also quite widespread here in Europe. This is not the place or time to expound on this theme. It is important, however, to acknowledge the *skandalon* and to testify that God, by his completely free self-revelation, has pledged himself to Israel forever. His revelation is at the same time a promise, to which God remains faithful. All peoples of all ages have had to and still must turn to Israel: Only there does his name dwell, and from there his promise goes out to all the world, to all peoples. The Feast of the Epiphany (January 6) testifies that "'the full number of the nations' now takes its 'place in the family of the patriarchs,' and ... [is] 'made worthy of the heritage of Israel'" (cf. CCC 528; [PL 54:242]).

This certainty about God's lasting fidelity to the people that, among all the peoples of the earth, is the bearer of God's name is inseparably connected with the certainty that Jesus of Nazareth is the Messiah of Israel, "the Son of the living God" (Mt 16:16). Jesus Christ is not only one manifestation of God alongside many others, but rather God's name in Person. It is important here to examine in greater depth many other things of which the world is only beginning to become aware since the twentieth century—especially through the horrors of the Shoah: that the uniqueness of Jesus that we Christians profess is inseparably connected with the uniqueness of Israel, for Jesus is "the light for revelation to the Gentiles and for glory to your people Israel" (Lk 2:32).

The Greek translators—long before Christ—rendered the name of God that was revealed in the burning bush with *ego eimi ho on* ("I am he who is"). This translation has been very controversial. Some say that it is a "Hellenization" and thus a philosophical falsification of the Divine Name, which above all is an expression of God's nearness and fidelity and is not meant as a general philosophical definition of God's Being. Yet such polemics often overlook the magnificent, consoling meaning of this translation: God proves to be the "I am here" precisely by virtue of the fact that he, unlike us, neither wavers nor passes away: heaven and earth "will perish, but *you endure*; they will all wear out like a garment ... but you are the same, and your years have no end" (Ps 102:26–27). With him "there is no variation or shadow due to change" (Jas 1:17); "God is 'He who Is,' from everlasting to everlasting, and as such remains ever faithful to himself and to his promises" (CCC 212). "The revelation of the ineffable name "I Am who Am" contains then the truth that God alone IS.... God is the fullness of Being and of every perfection, without origin and without end. All creatures receive all that they are and have from him; but he alone *is* his very being, and he is of himself everything that he is" (CCC 213).

How close the personal and the "ontological" meanings of the Divine Name come to each other is shown by something the Lord said to Saint Catherine of Siena (d. 1380): "You are she who is not; I am he who is." He added that if she pondered this word, she would be happy.

We, too, will be happy if we ponder this and take it to heart: he alone *is*; we have received our being and our life. The famous words of Saint Teresa of Avila (d. 1582) tell us what comfort there is in this philosophical truth:

> Let nothing trouble you / Let nothing frighten you
> Everything passes / God never changes
> Patience / Obtains all
> Whoever has God / Wants for nothing
> God alone is enough. (CCC 227)

3. A third consequence: If God's name is unique, then the name of man is unique also and distinctive. The God who reveals himself speaks to man, calls him by name: "Moses, Moses!" (Ex 3:4). Everyone has his name: "From the womb ... of my mother he called my name" (Is 49:1).

If God were a nameless and therefore "anonymous" power, then men, too, would be merely anonymous waves on the vast ocean of being. The fact that man is a person, distinctive, unrepeatable, endowed with an inalienable dignity, has its basis in the fact that he is God, the unique, distinctive One, who calls every person into existence. He is the first and last Thou of every man.

When God reveals his name, then that is a promise: "I will be the 'I am'." We, though, can answer as Moses answers

God's call at the burning bush: "Here am I!" (Ex 3:4). In this answer there is likewise a promise: "My heart is steadfast, O God, my heart is steadfast" (Ps 57:7). The ability to promise is, as we have seen, the unmistakable property of the person. In my perpetually new acceptance and free appropriation of what I have promised and of the purpose to which I have thereby shaped myself—"Behold, I am the handmaid of the Lord" (Lk 1:38)—I realize my humanity, my personal being.

Whereas God, of course, is completely identical to his name, we undergo the painful experience of infidelity, broken promises, sin. That, however, is precisely when God's name proves to be salvation and deliverance. Anyone who calls upon God's name is saved; he who is the expiation for all sin (cf. Jn 1:29; 1 Jn 2:2) will not reject anyone who calls upon the name of Jesus. The first to be saved was a criminal who repented and called upon the name of God, whom he experienced in the crucified King of the Jews: "Jesus, remember me when you come in your kingly power" (Lk 23:42). We, too, ask this: Father, hallowed be thy name: *Jesus.*

"Blessed are those who mourn, for they shall be comforted" (Mt 5:4)

A Dominican confrere, who had been stricken with bone cancer and suffered terrible pain, told me shortly before his liberating death, "Never speak carelessly about suffering. You have no idea what it is like." He was probably right about that. What do I know about the suffering of another? And how can I even imagine it, as long as I have not experienced it myself?

Too often the grief, affliction, and tears of our neighbor leave us dismayed and helpless; they are painful to us and make us embarrassed. In our major cities we hurry past places where suffering and misfortune become manifest. One image has been engraved unforgettably on my memory: It was in the year 1977 on the occasion of a short visit to Hong Kong. I was taking the famous ferry between Kowloon and Hong Kong, which is used daily by thousands of passengers. Then just in front of the pier, where a mass of humanity was waiting for the next boat, I saw a howling woman crouching on the ground. She was weeping and wailing; it was a glimpse of unspeakable misery, the way she desperately lifted up her hands from time to

March 14, 2004 (Third Sunday of Lent), Lenten homily, Notre Dame de Paris. Original text: "Heureux les affligés, car ils seront consolés" (Mt 5, 5); translated into English from the German translation by Elisabeth Heresch.

time, thereby making her face visible, which was marked by pain and suffering. No one paid any attention to her, and when the boat arrived and discharged an immense number of people, so as to take on the ones who were waiting, this entire mass of humanity walked past that woman who had dissolved into tears, without so much as giving her a glance. Finally I, too, walked past her, yet I simply cannot forget that scene.

When will they be comforted?

Has that poor woman from Hong Kong meanwhile had her comfort, here on earth or in the hereafter? We hope so, we believe it—even if it is only in the hereafter. Yet Jesus seems to be speaking not just about a perfectly happy hereafter. Where is the happiness of the sorrowing now? A happiness that is promised exclusively for a life in the future aroused the suspicion of Karl Marx (d. 1883), and not without reason. A life of blessedness that exists only in the form of a promise, he said, was the "opium of the people", a sort of drug that serves to make them forget their present suffering without doing anything about it.

With respect to many sorts of suffering, what progress we can see! Modern times have not waited for the comforting of those who mourn that is promised in heaven. Instead, modern man has resolutely set out to fight suffering, and the success of this battle is in fact notable. My confrere, who died twenty years ago from a horrible case of bone cancer, would certainly not have suffered so much today. There have been tremendous developments since then in methods of pain relief. No doubt physical suffering, although not conquered, has still been reduced considerably in our world today—at least in the West. And we have every reason to be glad about that. It is difficult for us to imagine how hard the lot of physical sufferings must have been that befell everyone in our society before our era. Maybe people were more rugged then, more accustomed to enduring sorrows. Maybe, too, our ability to bear physical pain has diminished sharply. Yet in any case it is comforting to know that in our time most sorts of pain can be brought under control.

That, incidentally, is one reason (although certainly not the most weighty) to oppose resolutely all attempts to legalize euthanasia. It is per se and in every respect unacceptable. The *Catechism of the Catholic Church* is quite clear in this regard: "Intentional euthanasia, whatever its forms or motives, is murder. It is gravely contrary to the dignity of the human person and to the respect due to the living God, his Creator" (CCC 2324). The *Catechism* explains, moreover, that "discontinuing medical procedures that are ... extraordinary, or disproportionate to the expected outcome can be legitimate", and it adds, concerning palliative therapy, that "palliative care is a special form of disinterested charity" (CCC 2278–79).

Again and again Europe attempts to legalize euthanasia, and one of the essential reasons alleged for it is that unbearable sufferings justify putting an end to one's life. I am happy, nevertheless, to be able to say that in Austria all the parties represented in Parliament have agreed to commit themselves neither in principle nor in practice to euthanasia but rather to choose the path of accompanying the dying, along the lines of the "hospice movement" that comes from England. I consider this agreement a fine example of what progress means. Indeed, in this instance medical progress is completely at the service of a human and Christian vision of man and of his destiny. "Blessed are those who mourn." I go so far as to regard dealing with incurable diseases and the end of earthly life as a very concrete form of putting this Beatitude into practice. It would be extremely desirable if the entire European Union,

all of Europe, would subscribe to this Austrian political agreement, which is ultimately a social agreement. And I invite
everyone, Christians and people of goodwill, to become
involved in this cause and to resist unwaveringly the drift toward
euthanasia. Europe must never forget what it has experienced in the past—the consequences of a racist ideology that
actively propagated euthanasia as a method of "racial hygiene".
This Europe, which for thirty years now has single-mindedly
been going down the path of legalizing "euthanasia" at the
beginning of human life and has already shaken human existence to its foundations by this breach in the dike, is now running the risk of digging a similarly catastrophic pit with the
legalization of euthanasia.

Why do I insist on this example? Because it shows in an
exemplary way that progress in the fight against suffering
cannot do away with death but can give a more humane
form to its arrival. To mitigate pain and to make death more
worth living (if you allow me this paradoxical way of putting it) is one of the positive aspects of what our time has
made possible. But is that the meaning that Jesus gave to
suffering, if he calls blessed those afflicted by suffering and
those who weep? Ground has been gained in the fight against
the physical evils of human life, but has it been at the expense
of the gospel? Did not Jesus encourage us to carry the cross
of our sufferings? Is he a preacher of human progress, or is
he not promising instead the conversion of sorrow, suffering, and all the pain of human life into its opposite?

Certainly, Christianity is not to be equated in a facile
way with a certain capacity for suffering, the glorification
of suffering, indeed, the negation of joy in life. Friedrich
Nietzsche (d. 1900) proposed that as his chief argument
against Christianity.

In fact, the Beatitudes are permanently inscribed in the char-
ter for Christian life as the essence of Christ's teaching, and

they express the exact opposite of such an attitude. They are a great and unparalleled promise of happiness. They promise happiness not only in the hereafter, but also *from now on*. The passive form of the promises ("they shall be comforted", "they shall be satisfied") indicates the divine action, in the Hebraic manner that avoids pronouncing the name of God: "God himself will comfort them." This promise of consolation, of happiness, comes from God, but it by no means leads to quietism, a passive attitude on the part of man.

The Beatitudes in the Gospel have stirred up a tremendous wave of active love of neighbor, inspiring collaboration in the divine plan of human happiness. How many initiatives for peace and reconciliation have resulted from the promise of blessings upon peacemakers! How many steps toward greater justice have resulted from the promise of blessedness to those who thirst for righteousness!

"Blessed are those who mourn, for they shall be comforted." This Beatitude is not meant to be confined to seeing one's neighbor suffer. Nor is it the glorification of tearful despair. It is the promise of an unending consolation by God, who "will wipe away every tear from their eyes" (Rev 21:4; Is 25:8). For this promise is a summons to anticipate that comfort—in fragmentary fashion, to be sure, but really. This promise does not allow us to be resigned to the tears of those who mourn and suffer. It challenges us to imitate God, who dries those tears. It is the definitive No to despair. It is the refusal to accept desolation as the last word about an unbearable life.

Has not the history of Christian life worthy of the name been characterized throughout the centuries by mighty efforts to fulfill this promise here and now? Mother Teresa (d. 1997), for example, did not resign herself to seeing people die who had succumbed to the misery of their *karma*. Mother Teresa tried to comfort them with the promise that they would die as human beings, as her brothers and sisters. She managed to accommodate the dying by a simple gesture, to let them sense—if only for a moment—that blessedness is meant for them.

The old hospitals, for instance the Hôtel-Dieu in Beaune [France], which tourists visit today, are testimonials to this promise of blessedness, for they testify that they were always a source of compassion, generosity, and active care for the sick. Since God the Lord identified himself with the sick and suffering (cf. Mt 25), the sick were regarded in the hospitals as having been especially favored by God, as his representatives on earth, and to serve them was a service to Christ, their Brother. The saintly Padre Pio was a shining example with respect to these promises. The countless penitents to whom he gave the gift bestowed by the risen Christ, the forgiveness of sins—how many of them experienced after all the comfort promised to the suffering!

The Church of Jesus, Mother of Consolation—is she not the one who makes this Beatitude a reality, every day, through the gift of her sacraments? The forgiveness of sins—what comfort could be more powerful? The gift of the Body and Blood of Christ—it is, truly, already here and now that she is comforting those who suffer. And finally the entire presence— invisible and yet so effective—of the Holy Spirit, the Comforter, who is given to us in the Church, where what Jesus promised to the suffering is put into action here and now.

If the Church is the Mother of Consolation, she is so through her *beauty* as well. In places where the desolation of ruined churches does not yet prevail, where the church is still a house that welcomes the visitor with a warming fire, where Jesus is still in the tabernacle, the expectation of all our grief, the acceptance of all our tears, in places where the churches are not yet closed, where we can enter into the space that breathes silence and bow before him who mysteriously dwells therein: this can become a moment of intense experience in which someone who is mourning is in fact comforted and our churches are once again that sublime refuge of the blessedness of tears that have been consoled. Yet in order for that to happen, we must do everything possible to keep them open, so that we can entrust our sufferings to him, Jesus, who is really present there. And what happiness it is to pour out tears in his presence; to encounter him whose glance so unsettled Peter after he had denied him! The tears of Peter, elicited by the unspeakable acceptance in Jesus' glance—therein lies, does it not, the happiness that Jesus promised!

So much for an initial look at the Beatitude about those who suffer. This Beatitude does not leave us idle and unmoved by other people's suffering—far from it! Instead, it constantly inspires new forms of comforting:

- Mitigating suffering by sympathy and compassion, concern and caring, and through the tireless fight against evils of every sort, physical and spiritual;
- Opening up the channels of consolation that God gave his Church in superabundance, so that she might be Mother and dispenser;
- Finding our way back to the beauty in which God's goodness is reflected, the refuge of comfort in the countless sufferings of this earthly life.

In a word, the Beatitudes are not a vague promise of another happiness found only in the hereafter. They are the anticipation of eternal happiness, which begins in this world.

To what kind of mourning does the promise of comfort apply?

When Jesus promises comfort to those who suffer, mourn, and weep, what sort of grief is meant? Any sort? Or only a certain kind? Is there this kind of weeping and that kind; can there be "good" and "bad" tears? Is there such a thing, then, as the refusal of comfort, as in the case of Rachel, who "is weeping for her children; she refuses to be comforted ... , because they are not" (Jer 31:15; cf. Mt 2:18)? Is there a pain so great that no comfort seems capable of reaching it—is that not the pain of the Shoah?

Everything we could mention here is only a small part of this enormous whole that constitutes the world of emotions and "passions" (in the classical sense of the word). The modern way of thinking puts only a few means at our disposal to analyze, evaluate, and master this wealth of human feelings. The Cartesian world view knew about thought, mind, and reason. The universe of the emotions ends up in the machinery of the physical mechanism. Consequently it is not surprising that moralists were rather uninterested in feelings or the moral aspect of our emotional nature. Moral obligation, for example in Kant, further reinforced this tendency by bringing human inclinations and urges into disrepute.

In contrast to that are the discourses of the great classical philosophers, both pagan and Christian. They accord an important status to the moral aspect of suffering and experiencing passions. Indeed, in determining the moral value of our human acts, their "emotional environment" is not insignificant and should be taken into consideration. Do our feelings express the straightforwardness of the heart? Are they in harmony with reality? My tears of joy or sadness are not simply physical reactions, merely mechanical reflexes, as the "behaviorists" with their materialistic understanding of the human psyche would view them. They are modes of expressing human qualities. They give more or less forceful expression to the moral nature of our doing and being. They are "appropriate" or not. If I responded to news about the death of my mother by making jokes, it would be correct to say that my reaction did not correspond to the reality. One would rightly be shocked by it. The angry tears of a child who does not get the candy he wants do not bode well for the character of that little person. They call for a strict upbringing. To console the child by giving in to his wish is certainly not the comfort that Jesus is talking about.

The sorrow of King Ahab over Naboth's refusal to give him his vineyard is not a neutral feeling. The king's desire is thwarted, and he finds it hard to cope with this disappointment—so hard that it ends in the murder of Naboth (1 Kings 21). In a moral analysis of the crime that King Ahab and his wife Jezebel have committed, the king's sorrow over an unfulfilled desire plays a major role. Is this the sorrow that Jesus promises to comfort? In this case the comfort consists, on the contrary, in the fact that Ahab repents when the prophet Elijah confronts him with the reality of his sin: God accepts this sorrow and lessens the punishment (1 Kings 21:27–29).

When Jesus encounters the funeral procession at the city gate of Nain and sees the tears of the widow who is burying her only son, his reaction perfectly corresponds to the reality. "And when the Lord saw her, he had compassion on her and said to her, 'Do not weep'" (Lk 7:13). Saint Luke speaks here about a deep feeling that, according to the ancients, was seated in the entrails, the "bowels of mercy". This compassion of Jesus, we must not forget, is the compassion of the incarnate God, the Word made flesh; it is the mercy of God that is reflected in the feeling of a heart, down to the human "bowels". The comfort that radiates from the gestures, words, and feelings of Jesus is the comfort of God himself, transferred and made accessible through the Incarnation of Jesus.

The Incarnation of Jesus: What a school for our wounded world of feelings! By watching Jesus, by following him, sensing his glance, and allowing himself to be led by him, the disciple of Jesus receives a true "education in feelings". Jesus' teaching is carried out equally through the follower's words and through his sentiments. "Have this mind among yourselves [*Hoc sentite in vobis*], which was in Christ Jesus", Paul demands (Phil 2:5).

What kind of sorrow is meant, then, in the Beatitude about those who need comforting? If feelings are not neutral but are to be weighed ethically, what sort of grief qualifies for the promised comfort?

Father Marie-Joseph Le Guillou (d. 1990), who for years had Parkinson's disease and therefore truly knew what suffering is, was able to say: "First of all, let us cast off a very widespread ambivalence: Weeping has to do with retreating into oneself. Many people weep, but many people do not comprehend that the tears they have shed signify a self-enclosure, so that they cannot open themselves up to God and to others. There are tears that allow us to see only ourselves and prevent us from seeing reality as our Lord sees it." [1]

Following Saint Paul, masters of the spiritual life distinguish the sadness that withdraws into itself from the sadness that opens itself up to God and neighbor. The one is a failing, the other—a virtue. We should fight against the one and strive for the other. Man becomes sad when he loses something that is dear to him: someone who was close to him, health, material goods, reputation, peace of mind, and so on. Nevertheless, one must choose here between two paths: that of retreating into oneself and the path to life.

[1] Marie-Joseph Le Guillou, *Qui ose encore parler de bonheur?* (Paris, 1991), 54.

Nothing is more dangerous than self-pity, the temptation to commiserate with oneself. One then sees only one's own misery, which becomes, so to speak, a prison that keeps one away from others. It isolates a person and leads finally to despair. It deprives the suffering person of the joy of life. "It is like a poisoned arrow that strikes not only the body but also the soul", says Saint John Chrysostom.[2] The spiritual fathers recommend a very simple test in order to diagnose whether this arrow has already pierced our soul: Does the success of someone else make me sad, or does it cheer me? Envy and jealousy are indications of a mistaken sadness.

The other sadness, which the Fathers call the *charapoion penthos*, the "sadness that causes joy",[3] enters into our life through the narrow gate of repentance. The Christian interpretation of the Beatitudes of Jesus unanimously confirms that the first sadness to which the promise of comfort applies is the sadness that bewails its own sins—not out of regret or disappointment with oneself, however, but because the heart has encountered him who forgives.

We find the prototype of this blessedness in the tears of Simon Peter after his threefold denial of his Master, to whom he had promised that he would give his life for him. The gaze of Jesus! That gaze which nothing will ever erase from Peter's memory: "And he went out and wept bitterly" (Lk 22:62). These are the tears that give life. These are the tears that leave indescribable happiness in the heart. These tears are like a new birth. Anyone who has really experienced it will confirm this. And he will agree with the remark by Saint Ephrem the Syrian (d. 373): "A face streaming with tears has an indescribable beauty." [4] "Blessed are those who weep": *These* are the tears that bring happiness.

[2] Saint John Chrysostom, *Letter to Olympias* 10, 2; SC 13bis, 246ff.
[3] John Climacus, *Ladder to Heaven*, 7.
[4] Saint Ephrem the Syrian, *Sermo asceticus* 1.

These tears contain within them the promised comfort on one condition: that they are prompted by a new look at reality and flow out of an acceptance of the truth. It means the end of evasions, deceptive appearances, and false excuses. It gives reality and truth back to us again. The happiness in sadness about one's own sins consists largely of this. The Samaritan woman in her encounter with Jesus represents a shining example of this Beatitude. Even though the Gospel does not mention tears, this woman is no doubt grieving. Otherwise she would not be going to Jacob's well at an unusual time, at noon, in the broiling heat of the middle of the day. You see, only at that hour can she be certain that she will not meet anyone from her town. She is ashamed of her disorderly life, and this isolates her, shuts her up behind the walls of the judgments that surround her. Jesus himself addresses her. He asks her for water and makes the first breach in her reticence.

> "Go, call your husband, and come here."
> "I have no husband."
> "You are right in saying, 'I have no husband'; for you have had five husbands, and he whom you now have is not your husband; this you said truly."

Now here is the surprising thing. The woman hurries into the town and calls to the people, "Come, see a man who told me all that I ever did. Can this be the Christ?" (Jn 4:7, 16–18, 29).

What a liberation: Finally, someone tells me everything I have done. And see, all at once I emerge from isolation, I find myself in the company of people, from whom my failings and sins have isolated me. "The truth will make you free" (Jn 8:32), Jesus had promised. It is exactly the opposite of what we fear: If people know the whole truth about me, I will be condemned by everyone. Therefore I must keep my faults hidden and make sure that the truth does not come to light. And in order to do that, it is better to shift the blame onto others, to make my neighbor the center of attention, to expose his faults and accuse him so as to defend myself. That is the strategy of the "children of this world", with all their baggage of the sadness and grief of this world.

The Beatitude about those who mourn breaks through this closed circle. It promises comfort and joy to anyone who no longer accuses his neighbor but rather looks for guilt in himself. Sadness about our own sins, about our misery as sinners, allows us to be liberated from the illusions we fabricate about ourselves and the world. Repentance, a contrite heart, allows us to see our human condition in a clear and living light. Now we can agree with what Christians of an earlier time used to say about this world, that it is a "valley of tears". The ideology of the '68 generation rejected such metaphors as too bleak and not optimistic enough.

Yet it is quite true that earthly life makes us walk through a valley of tears. Far from being pessimistic, this image, which is taken from the famous hymn *Salve Regina*, is a perfect translation of the Beatitude we have been considering. Let us stay with the metaphor: a valley, certainly, can be narrow, gloomy, and wearisome. But it also contains two elements of hope: first, it has a direction. Someone who goes through a valley is not walking around in circles. The valley leads to the wide world. This image is different from the image of the wheel of fate, which revolves endlessly. Secondly, the valley is open to the sky above. Someone who moves forward in the valley will always have over him the promise of heaven.

But there is more to it than these two elements of openness. In this valley of tears we have heard a promise: the promise of comfort. The Greek word for it is *paraklethéson-tai* ("... they will be comforted"). Literally the word *par-akalein* (in its passive form) means "to be called to someone's side". *Desolatio*—"being disconsolate"—means being reduced to complete loneliness. *Consolatio*—"comfort"—implies, in contrast, someone who enters into my loneliness so as to share it with me. God comforts us, not by removing all need, all misery, and all difficulties, but rather by bringing himself into the picture and by sharing them with us. God transforms this valley of tears by becoming our closest friend. Our loneliness is no longer desolation, since the Son of God has become our Brother. Who eventually comforted the woman in tears in the harbor in Hong Kong? Her pain must have been so great that only the closeness of the incarnate God could have comforted her. Is she still on this earth? Of one thing I am certain in faith: God did not walk past her tears. He dried them upon her arrival at her port of destination. And perhaps there was someone there, too, even before she began her final voyage, who could tell her that the promise applied especially to her: "Blessed are those who mourn, for they shall be comforted."

"Teacher, where are you staying?"

Europe Can Rediscover Itself

The future belongs to those who find reasons to pin their hopes on the younger generations. The following pages are about this hope and the reasons for it, especially with regard to Europe.

What a surprise for France the "World Youth Day" in Paris in August 1997 was! Who would have believed that so many young people from Europe and all over the world would set out on a journey to come and hear Pope John Paul II, who was already bent over by age and illness, to pray and celebrate with him, so as to profess their faith and give joyful expression to it?! Who would have thought that just as many young French people would join their companions who had come in great numbers from Spain, Italy, and so many other countries of the world? There are so many explanations that could be improvised, yet the happening itself remains a big surprise. Considered as an isolated event, it could all be just a big flash in the pan. Yet since the World Youth Day in Rome during the Holy Year 2000, that explanation is no longer possible. Great perplexity reigns among the commentators: How are we to understand this phenomenon? The Pope invites

March 4, 2001 (First Sunday of Lent), Lenten homily, Notre Dame de Paris. Original text: "Maître, où demeures-tu?—L'Europe peut retrouver son lieu"; translated into English from the German translation by Elisabeth Heresch.

young people, and they come, in even greater numbers than to Paris. More than two million young people on the university campus in Tor Vergata, at the night vigil, and at the great concluding Mass. Observers were speechless, astounded at the long waiting line of young people who patiently inched forward so as to walk through the Holy Door of Saint Peter's Basilica or to enter one of the six hundred confessional booths in the Circus Maximus. How can this be reconciled with the received wisdom about secularization that says that once religion is lost, there is no turning back?

The Holy Year, the Great Jubilee of the Year 2000, seems to testify to the exact opposite.

With unwavering determination Pope John Paul II has been marching toward this Jubilee Year since the beginning of his pontificate. With a sort of stubbornness that we call hope, he has ceaselessly invited the whole Church to cross the threshold of hope. Caution: he is talking about hope, not about some kind of naïve optimism. It is talk about a firm conviction, anchored in God alone, that Christ is the same yesterday, today, and always and that after Easter, despite all appearances to the contrary, there is every reason to hope. Before our eyes stood a man who in an extraordinary way radiated the power of hope. Is this the deeper reason for the attractiveness of Pope John Paul II among so many young people? For surely he was the one who truly was able to give reasons for hope; he was the one who spoke to the hearts of the youth.

What gives Europe reasons to hope? It is about this that I would like to talk—and perhaps even provide evidence. The former president of the European Commission, Jacques Delors, often spoke about the need *to give Europe a soul.* His successors never tired of taking up this slogan again and again. I think it a question not so much of giving Europe a soul as of rediscovering it. Europe has a soul, and this is what enlivens the continent. Although it is true that it is in such great danger that one might think it was completely gone, it is nevertheless true also that it is alive and is only waiting to be rediscovered.

When we speak about today's Europe, that often means— and with good reason—speaking about the dangers it faces and its maladies, the tragedies of abortion and declining birth rates, immigration, cultural conflicts, atomic and genetic threats, and much more. Although we will not talk much about those things here, this is not out of complacency or ignorance but rather out of the deep conviction that only those who give reasons for hope can also manage effectively to heal Europe's ills, her bodily and spiritual wounds.

Reasons for hope

Come, then, friends, "come and see" what the great prophet of hope, John Paul II, showed us. A scene from the Gospel of John takes us to the first beginnings of the Christian adventure. It is important to relive this hour of beginning, the first moment of the encounter with Jesus, the place where everything began on the day when great hope began. I take up now this meditation suggested by John Paul II.

One day John the Baptist, surrounded by his disciples, sees Jesus walking by on Jordan's bank and says, "Behold the Lamb of God." The scene is repeated the next day. Now two disciples separate themselves from the group and prepare to follow Jesus. He turns around and asks, "What do you seek?" "Teacher, where are you staying?" The two youths answer with a question because they are somewhat embarrassed and do not know how they should start the conversation. "Come and see", is Jesus' answer. What happened next was remembered precisely by one of the two, the author of the Gospel, who calls himself "the disciple whom Jesus loved": "They came and saw where he was staying; and they stayed with him that day, for it was about the tenth hour" (Jn 1:35–39), four o'clock in the afternoon. The Apostle recalls this detail even in his old age as he is writing his Gospel. Unforgettable is the hour of the first encounter! He tells us nothing about what happened during that hour which was so decisive for his life or about what Jesus discussed with them or what they felt at that moment. This first encounter remains a mystery. But one thing becomes clear, when on the next day Andrew, the second of the two, meets his brother Simon, whom Jesus would call *Kephas*, Peter, and says to him, "We have found the Messiah" and brings him to Jesus (Jn 1:40–42). "We have found!" What an expression! "What do you seek?" asked Jesus. And after that first encounter, they can say "We have found!"

In John's recollection, those first hours, which were to define his whole life, conceal a mysterious meaning. Enriched by the entire experience of a lifetime shaped by Jesus, he attributes multiple meanings to this scene: on the one hand, the short, simple dialogue between the two young men and Jesus; on the other hand, the momentousness of the mystery that it contains. "What do you seek?"—words that go deeper than just a superficial question about momentary circumstances: What do you want? What is it basically that you are seeking? For what are you striving? What is the desire in your inmost heart? Do you know it already? And the question with which they reply—"Teacher where are you staying?"—is that not a much more far-reaching question than a simple question about an address? Where do you dwell? Where is your "place", "the place where you rest", where your heart is at home, where the source of your life is; where is that secret place from which you come and from which you speak? "Come and see!" The whole adventure of their life of following Jesus will be an ever deeper "Come and see"; they will discover more and more where Jesus stays, where his secret place is, and they will truly know that he dwells "in the Father" and the Father in him, that God himself is this place from which he comes and to which he is leading them when he invites them to be with him. They themselves will also have *found*, through him and in him, what they were seeking. The One whom their hearts were seeking without really knowing it, "the Messiah", the One whom their people Israel was expecting, the One who was to fulfill the longing of the peoples: Truly, we have found, they will be able to say: We have found him.

The Holy Father suggested to the youth from all over the world that they reflect on this scene so that they might discover what the deepest desire of their heart is. They should come to see him who is calling them so as to find and become acquainted with the Messiah of their life, so as then to be able to say to others: "We have found the Messiah", and to lead them to Jesus.

Is it not time for us also to turn back to the beginnings of the Christian adventure, which became an integral component of Europe's path through history? This spring has not dried up; it is flowing abundantly, the spring of the Gospel, which the two young men discovered when they walked with Jesus and, in so doing, had the privilege of seeing where he stayed. This earliest beginning remains present before our eyes, and this presence makes it possible to rediscover the place where the Teacher stays, the place to which he is leading us, so that we might no longer be homeless and so that we can find "Europe's soul".

The Europe of the shrines

Come and see the shrines of France, of Europe, those sacred places of prayer and of rediscovered hope! I recall a little book by my confrere the Dominican Père Serge Bonnet, which caused quite a stir in the seventies: *Prières secrètes des français d'aujourd'hui* [Secret prayers of French people today]. Whereas the theory of secularization dominated almost all the faculty in theology and sociology departments, and popular religion was declared to be wasting away, behold— Père Bonnet presented the results of a broad-based sociological study of the books of "prayer intentions" from the most important sacred places in France. The results blatantly contradicted the theory of secularization that was prevalent then: not only do French people today pray a lot, but this is true about French people of all age groups, having all levels of education and from every social class, who are observed coming to pray at places of pilgrimage—and they pray about every joy and sorrow that human life brings with it. Quite a few sociologists today think that the theory of the increasing secularization of the modern world is no longer tenable.[1] Père Bonnet no longer stands alone.

Come and see these places of prayer! The soul of Europe is there. Even though the crisis of priestly and religious vocations has affected extensive regions of Europe (without necessarily being irreversible, as numerous examples from major cities like Paris, Rome, or Madrid show us), the trend of turning to contemplation undeniably continues. How many of the centers of monastic life in France have been replenished in the last three decades! The Europe of the monasteries, of the shrines, is a reality. It suffices to come and see in order to be convinced of it.

But I am by no means forgetting the less visible places of prayer. My revered spiritual father during the time of my

[1] For literature on secularization, see R. Stark, "Secularization, R.I.P.", *Sociology of Religion* 60/3 (1999): 249–73; Peter L. Berger, ed., *The Desecularization of the World: Resurgent Religion and World Politics* (Grand Rapids: William B. Eerdmans Publishing, 1999).

studies in Paris and Saulchoir, Fr. Martin Hubert, O.P. (d. 1976), told me that there is no place in Paris where people pray so much as in the Metro [subway]. I might add "and in the hospitals". *Secret prayers of French people today*: I am thinking also about the prayers of our many Muslim fellow citizens and those of others. . . .

I am not anxious about a Europe that prays!

Churches, open your doors!

"Come and see" the infinitely many holy places in this Europe, which has not lost its soul but perhaps has only forgotten it somewhat. I am inspired by a very simple idea, which nevertheless could have far-reaching consequences: How many churches, also in the sense of church buildings, are there in Europe? I do not know. I only know that the Archdiocese of Vienna alone numbers around twelve hundred. Each one is a *Gotteshaus*, as we say, a "house of God", "a place where God dwells among men". But how sad it is to see them so often neglected, abandoned, devastated—but most frequently closed. I present here an appeal and a fervent request: Do not leave your churches in this condition! Open the doors of your churches! Realize again what a treasure your churches are in your midst. What a comfort it is to be able to step inside a church and pray there in silence, to feel close to God, and to know that he is near us! I know, of course, that there are so many obstacles to overcome: proprietary questions, the fear of vandalism and theft, which unfortunately is all too legitimate, and other factors as well. Yet all these problems can be solved, provided we are profoundly convinced of the incalculable value of these oases, these places where the soul can breathe freely. I imagine little associations, resembling the medieval confraternities, that would make it their goal to take care of the church in their town or district and to make sure that it was open and guarded; in doing so they themselves would benefit from the prayer time that their duties afforded them, while they would unobtrusively be available to help those who came to the church looking for refuge, consolation, and assistance from on high.

A unique presence: The Real Presence

"Teacher, where are you staying?" "He is there", Saint John Vianney, the Curé of Ars (d. 1859), liked to say during his catecheses. "He is there", he would say, while turning toward the tabernacle. In the simplicity that our faith gives us, I repeat this statement by the Curé of Ars. The Teacher is here, in this humble and hidden but entirely real presence of the Eucharist. Frère Roger Schutz (d. 2005) of Taizé wrote in his diary, while describing the little Romanesque church of the village of Taizé in Bourgogne where he especially liked to say his prayers: "This place is inhabited." Indeed, so many places all over Europe are inhabited, pervaded by a unique presence of the One who desired to be in our midst in the unassuming form of bread that has become his Body. How can we bear to leave a church closed when the Teacher himself dwells there? Certainly, he himself said, "I am with you always, to the close of the age" (Mt 28:20); he is present in many ways, and we experience his presence above all through faith in him. But how can anyone not be spellbound by this unique presence in what we call the "Real Presence", his presence par excellence? And how could we priests and pastors not do everything possible to ensure that our churches stay open all day and even at night, or at least sometimes?

Liturgical reform and the experience of God

"Teacher, where are you staying?" "Come and see!" When Saint Paul spoke about the liturgical gatherings in Corinth, he said that an unbeliever who happened to walk in would have to "fall on his face, worship God and declare that God is really among you" (cf. 1 Cor 14:25). That is precisely what the liturgical reform implemented in the wake of the Second Vatican Council intended to accomplish. There are few questions that divided Catholics so much after the Council as the liturgy—especially in France. The debates were passionate, the disagreements vehement, the rifts between the two sides deep and—unfortunately—lasting. Certainly the phase of excessive experimentation (with which I was acquainted from painful experience) appears by and large to be over. In many respects the liturgy has rediscovered a certain equilibrium; the pendulum has "swung back". From now on liturgical reform is part of the Church's life, and a return to the "old Mass" seems neither desirable nor possible for the great majority. Yet we cannot shut our eyes to a truth that seems obvious to me: the crisis in the liturgy is one factor—among many others—responsible for the dramatic decrease in the practice of the faith, in France and elsewhere. One would have to treat the problem at greater length so as to avoid drawing hasty conclusions. The fact is undeniable: the decline in religious practice is dramatic. But instead of trying to find sociological and other explanations for this phenomenon, I invite you: *Come and see* those positive experiences which show us the way we should follow. One fact in particular comes to mind after thirty-five years of observing (and enduring) the liturgical crisis: wherever the liturgy is celebrated in a dignified and beautiful manner, solemnly without opulence, prayerfully without sanctimony, the faithful not only do not drift away but even come back. I see an urgent need to cultivate and deepen what Romano Guardini and subsequently Joseph Ratzinger, our Holy Father Pope Benedict XVI, have called the "spirit of the liturgy".

Rediscovering the sense of God

Certainly, a Mass—even the most unpretentious or humble Mass, as far as its ceremonies are concerned—is still the Holy Sacrifice of the Mass and therefore infinitely precious. Yet that does not relieve us of our duty but rather enjoins us to devote special care to the liturgy, to the worship of God, since it concerns the most precious gift that has been entrusted to us. The "spirit of the liturgy" is above all *Gottesdienst*, "divine service", in a twofold sense: it is the worship of God, who comes to us, who is close to us and present to us here, and it is the service of man, who responds with his worship and praise. It seems to me that there is an urgent need to reflect on this significance of the liturgy, so that it might truly express and proclaim the *sursum corda*— "Lift up your hearts"—and thus raise hearts to the Thrice-Holy God. "Only the mystery consoles", Fr. Karl Rahner (d. 1984) once said. Only a liturgy that lifts up our hearts to God, who comes to us, will strengthen us in hope and comfort us with God's true consolation. Once again, so that there will be no misunderstanding: however humble a liturgy may be externally, it is still a Holy Mass. Nevertheless, concern for the beauty and dignity of the liturgy is a gesture of love and reverence, which we offer to him who comes to us through the sensible signs of the liturgy.

I have the good fortune and the privilege to serve the Church of God in Vienna, and it is for me a source of the utmost amazement to be able to pray here and to celebrate so often the major liturgical feasts to the music of Mozart,

Haydn, Schubert, and Bruckner—not only in Saint Stephen's Cathedral, but even in small parishes.

Rediscovering the beauty of the liturgy

What treasures there are to rediscover, not out of an archaeological interest, but rather for joy over the beauty of divine worship! The saintly Curé of Ars is well qualified to teach us this "spirit of the liturgy", since he made such great efforts to foster it. Mother Teresa once received a very valuable ruby as a gift. Spontaneously she said that it belonged on the tabernacle of her chapel in Calcutta. Someone objected that she could sell it instead and then give a lot of money to the poor. To which she replied, "If we neglect to honor Christ, we soon neglect the poor, too." The liturgy must pour out that pleasing fragrance that filled the whole house when Mary of Bethany, in a spontaneous gesture of love, poured oil of nard—which was especially costly—over Jesus' feet (cf. Jn 12:1–8). How much Europe owes to this "spirit of the liturgy"! Even though the products of this great treasure of divine worship have migrated from the church into concert halls, museums, scholarly studies, archaeology, and archives, the pleasing fragrance of that oil has not faded; at any moment it can awaken in the soul an intense desire to rediscover its source and to know him from whom this fragrance originates.

One indicator among many: the immense success of the exhibition of images of Christ in the National Gallery in London in the year 2000, entitled "Seeing Salvation". Come and see! These works of Christian art from practically all the major museums of London were almost all of liturgical origin. Within the context of divine worship, they not only were supposed to speak about events from the past, but also testified to their active presence: Christ the Redeemer, his angels and his saints in their saving and helping activity in the present time. Having made their way into museums and major collections of art, these are the works that ceaselessly touch hearts, even those of religious illiterates, the number of whom is constantly increasing in Europe. Although this illiteracy, this dramatic loss of the most elementary knowledge about the faith and Christian culture, is cause for concern, the endless waiting lines of visitors to the exhibition in London give us a glimpse of the great thirst today for the source of so much beauty.

The parallel is astounding: the long queues of people waiting outside the doors of a museum—the National Gallery in London—for the purpose of "Seeing Salvation", for the sake of all those works of art and images of Christ, and in the same year 2000 the long lines of pilgrims waiting to pass through another door, the "Holy Door", which symbolizes Christ the Redeemer, the Door of Life.

"What do you seek?" In seeing those long waiting lines, how could one not think of this question that Jesus posed two thousand years ago to the two young men? "Teacher, where are you staying?" Who are you, Teacher, Source of so much beauty, so much consolation? And how could one help thinking of the other request made to the Apostle Philip by several Greeks who were on pilgrimage to Jerusalem for the Paschal feast: "We wish to see Jesus!" (Jn 12:21)?

"Like those pilgrims of two thousand years ago, the men and women of our own day—often perhaps unconsciously—ask believers not only to 'speak' of Christ, but in a certain sense to 'show' him to them." [2] "To see Jesus"—that means above all to look into the mirror of the Gospel. It must be

---

[2] John Paul II, apostolic letter *Novo Millennio Ineunte*, January 6, 2001, no. 16.

said and repeated again and again: The countenance of Jesus of Nazareth is portrayed in the Gospels with such precision and fidelity that it is above all uncertainty. For me it is a source of amazement to read and reread the dramatic history of biblical criticism—from the late eighteenth century down to our day. Two hundred years of intensive historical criticism have not diminished the reliability of the Gospel accounts but, on the contrary, have reinforced their credibility by the historical exactness of the image they give us of Christ. Our faith in Jesus, Israel's Messiah, the Son of the living God, is based, not on myths or symbols, but rather on facts, the testimony of eyewitnesses who are reliable and who intended to convey to us nothing but what they had heard and seen with their own eyes, what their hands had touched—the Word of life (cf. 1 Jn 1:1).

I venture to add one more thing—at the risk of being taken for a fundamentalist. Surely you have seen photographs of the Shroud of Turin. You have seen that manly face which has been disfigured by torments, by the traces of his ordeals, which correspond in every detail to the account of Jesus' Passion. For a hundred years many, many scientific investigations have attempted to shed light on the origin of this image. I will not go into that here. I will simply say how moved I am by this mute testimony of the face, of the body of Jesus. And I think that it is especially significant that our time, which does not exactly have a wealth of modern artworks portraying Christ, has received from the hands of science, so to speak, this unique, inexplicable image that allows us—I make so bold as to think—to see Jesus.

In order to see Jesus and to recognize him, however, it is not enough to look at his picture, however authentic it may be. It is not enough to see Jesus; one must also learn *how to see Jesus*. And I would like to say a few more words about that to conclude this meditation.

"Come and see": the whole journey of Jesus with his disciples is to educate their way of seeing. By learning to see people and things, situations and what they call for, with his eyes, they become vessels of this creative and transformative power that Jesus radiates, which has contributed so much to giving Europe a soul. This gaze of Jesus, of the incarnate God, upon men "fully reveals man to himself" (*Gaudium et spes*, no. 22).

I will pick another—seemingly insignificant—scene from the Gospel so as to make clear how Jesus opens his disciples' eyes for his way of seeing. Once again Jesus says to them, "Come and see!" But what he shows them is rather surprising. He directs their attention to a poor old woman, a widow.

They are in the Temple in Jerusalem—a few days before his Passion. The little scene that follows encapsulates, so to speak, the essence of everything Jesus taught his followers. Jesus has taken a seat opposite the treasury. He watches the crowd as they put their offerings into the treasury, and many wealthy people put in large sums. "And a poor widow came, and put in two copper coins" (Mk 12:41–42). At that moment Jesus summons his disciples and says to them, "Truly, I say to you, this poor widow has put in more than all those who are contributing to the treasury. For they all contributed out of their abundance; but she out of her poverty has put in everything she had, her whole living" (Mk 12:43–44).

No one has noticed her, this poor old widow, neither the group of pilgrims nor the disciples of Jesus. He, Jesus, sees her. He who knows the hearts of men and knows what her donation is worth. He calls his disciples together to show them what they themselves have not seen: the true greatness of that widow.

By introducing them to his way of seeing, he teaches them what it means to be his disciples. He teaches them to see things, situations, and people with his eyes. This is how the Church comes about. She is and should be the community of those who see with the eyes of Jesus and who understand with his mind, who will with his will, who feel with his heart.

In showing them this poor old woman, he opens their eyes to the true greatness of man; he liberates their way of seeing from illusions and from being dazzled by the false ostentation of this world. "She ... has put in everything she had, her whole living", literally, "her whole life". Through this gift of the two small coins—"everything she had"—she becomes the image of what Jesus himself will do by giving "his whole life" for all mankind.

Jesus calls his disciples to him specifically to show them this woman, because what was at stake was a very great and important matter that they ought to see and understand. But we should pay attention to a significant detail: the woman herself does not notice anything, neither the fact that others have noticed her nor that her gesture is being praised. Jesus says nothing to her; he neither praises her nor promises a great reward. The gratuitousness of her gesture thereby becomes even more evident. No one would have paid her any attention, neither the rich people nor the crowds in the Temple nor the disciples, who—as so often—would have noticed nothing had the Teacher himself not pointed it out.

Jesus shows them this woman who does not know about her own greatness. He recommends to them the self-forgetfulness of those who do not act in order to "be praised by men" (Mt 6:2). This image will be impressed upon their hearts. By entering more deeply into Christ's way of seeing, they become acquainted with Jesus' joy, which exults over the action of God in the hearts of the little ones and of the poor. With Jesus they will be able to praise the Father, who has "revealed [these things] to infants" (Mt 11:25–26).

Finally, I venture to draw one conclusion: It was the school of Jesus' way of seeing and the lessons of his Heart that opened up for Europe so many paths of charity, created hospitals and orphanages, and inspired attentiveness to the poor of every kind. Sensing and knowing how Jesus sees the poor, how his glance seizes upon even the slightest gesture of magnanimity, countless disciples of Jesus have devised gestures and activities that are inspired by love of neighbor. Yet Jesus' admiration for those who give of themselves is not limited to those who know him. On the contrary—Jesus teaches his disciples to bow in respect before every act of love of neighbor, no matter who performs it, regardless of his religion or faith.

I would like to add this, too: the tremendous treasures of beauty that Christianity has brought forth ultimately have their origin in this school of seeing as Jesus sees. How can one imagine a work such as Michelangelo's *Pietà*, however talented the artist, if it were not also the work of a vision that had been formed by the human heart of the God-man?

But all that would probably be incomplete without one final point: Again it has always been Jesus' glance through which the Church has gained insight into her sins and also into where and how far she still falls short of what Jesus assigns her to see and to do. That was the reason why Pope John Paul II wanted to acknowledge the sins of the Church's children under the watchful eyes of Jesus on the Cross when, on March 12 in the year 2000, he asked God for forgiveness for the sins of Jesus' disciples.

When Peter had denied his beloved Teacher three times, the latter turned around and looked at him. That look was imprinted forever on Peter's heart. His eyes met Jesus' irreproachable glance, and in tears he received the invaluable gift of forgiveness.

That is the hope that sustains us. It allows us to go forward under the watchful eyes of Jesus. Come and see!

III

MAN

God Alone Is Great

Tribute to Otto von Habsburg

The blind man sitting beside the road from Galilee to Jerusalem, who insistently calls out to Jesus, loudly and clearly, "Lord, have mercy on me!" and who asks Jesus, "Let me receive my sight" (cf. Lk 18:38, 41), is an image of us all. Despite all our wisdom and experience, we always have to say: We are poor and blind, too. We must beseech the Lord, "Let me receive my sight", help me to see, open my eyes so that I might recognize what is right, and give me the strength to do it.

Otto von Habsburg is a man to whom God gave the power to see from the perspective of the Christian faith, even during years that were difficult for his family, for our land [Austria], and for the whole world.

Election and universality

The Book of Maccabees tells of a difficult and grim chapter in the history of God's people, when it was threatened

November 20, 2002, homily at the Mass of Thanksgiving on the occasion of the ninetieth birthday of Otto von Habsburg, Saint Stephen's Cathedral, Vienna. November 19, 2007, homily at the Eucharist celebrated on the occasion of the ninety-fifth birthday of Otto von Habsburg, Saint Stephen's Cathedral, Vienna.

These two homilies refer to the following passages from the Bible: Rev 4:1–11; Lk 19:11–28 (II.) and 1 Macc 1:10–15, 41–43, 54–57, 62–64; Lk 18:35–43 (I.).

with extinction, not for the first time and not for the last time in its dramatic history. It was his people, the people that God had chosen to be his own. But do not all peoples say, sooner or later in their history, that they are chosen? Is it not a primordial temptation of all nations to say, "We are God's people", a chosen people? Is it not a dangerous ideology that easily leads to totalitarianism when a people considers itself chosen? How much misery this idea of the chosen people has caused in the history of humanity, down to the extremely difficult and tragic twentieth century! And yet there is an essential difference here: the election of God's people Israel does not signify a demarcation from the others, not an exclusive status as opposed to all other nations; instead it is supposed to be a blessing for all peoples. Thus from the very beginning there was something universal in this election of the people of God, something that was then to become a reality in the Church, the new people of God: catholicity, that is, universality understood, not as a delimitation, but rather as existence for others. In choosing Israel, God's object was to bring his law—which is a way of life, freedom, and justice—to all peoples. Israel was to be, so to speak, the beacon on the path of righteousness and freedom for all peoples.

The universality of the great empires of that era was different, and it is so to this day. They are political attempts to achieve a kind of universality, not in variety, but rather in the imposition of uniformity on everyone else, in other words, the imperialistic idea of an empire in which all must be the same. Hence it has a compulsory form of worship. The Books of Maccabees give an account of how all peoples had been subjected to the compulsory worship of the empire ruled by the successors of Alexander the Great. All religions must be relativized so as to conform to the dictates of political unity. That results in what Pope

Benedict XVI has called the "dictatorship of relativism". They all comply except Israel. Only the chosen people puts up resistance, insists on the distinction, on the fact that it is different; it remains faithful to its God, lives out the distinction, and thus reserves the right to freedom. In Christ that will be fulfilled. So he introduced into history the saying that to this day discriminates between two sorts of universality, one totalitarian and the other freedom-oriented: "Render to Caesar the things that are Caesar's and to God the things that are God's" (Mt 22:21).

To this day two sorts of universalism collide with each other: the one that levels, relativizes, and equalizes everyone is a totalitarian universalism. The other one, inspired by Judeo-Christian revelation, which sees humanity as a family, takes as its premise what is written on the first page of the Bible, that "God created man in his own image and likeness" (cf. Gen 1:26–27), and thus gave man a dignity that no State and no authority can set aside, a dignity whose highest expression is religious freedom.

This look at the Book of Maccabees also says something essential about the efforts of Otto von Habsburg over many decades. We know that no earthly kingdom, not even the imperial line of which he is the worthy descendent, no kingdom on earth is the "kingdom of God". But some political realities come closer than others to what the kingdom of God ought to be among men. Some political realities do greater justice to that universality which the people Israel, which Judeo-Christian revelation makes present. I think that a look back into history allows us to say fairly that the Habsburg kingdom came closer to this open universality than many other political realities in European and world history. The fact that it was inspired by the Catholic faith certainly had something to do with it also. Today's European unification, to which Otto von

Habsburg has devoted himself with all his strength for decades, is an arduous attempt to come closer to that reality. But again and again [such] attempts run the risk of becoming, not open universality, but rather the totalitarian sort. Thus the dictatorship of relativism afflicts Europe, a dictatorship that tries to bring everything into line but that is ultimately unmasked inasmuch as it cannot really preserve respect for human dignity but goes so far as to allow the killing of the unborn, the elderly, and the handicapped.

Otto von Habsburg stands for an image of man and, thus, for an understanding of society and politics that is profoundly marked by the Judeo-Christian tradition. Nourished by this source, it is characterized by a great openness, a deep respect for variety and diversity, in the knowledge of the common interest of the one human family, of the people who have been created in God's image. The strength to actualize such a vision comes most profoundly from the Christian faith, from the deep spring of Christian discipleship.

Responsibility for Austria and Europe

"Dieu seul est grand."—"God alone is great." With these words, Massillon began his famous funeral sermon for King Louis XIV (d. 1715). There was probably no other royal house in the turbulent history of Europe that was so imbued with the truth of this remark as the Habsburg House: "Gott allein ist gross." When Empress Zita was buried on April 1, 1989, in the imperial vault of the Capuchin monastery, those in attendance experienced once again the moving ritual of the imperial ceremonial, according to which the body of the Empress was not admitted until all her sovereign titles had been left behind and it was only "a poor sinner" knocking at the door.

"God alone is great." A staggering vision of the greatness and holiness of God was granted to the seer of Patmos, and we too can see it, to a certain extent, in the words of the Revelation of John:

Holy, holy, holy
is the Lord God Almighty
who was and is and is to come! (Rev 4:8; cf. Is 6:3)

When we sing the Thrice-Holy hymn, before our Holy God becomes truly and really present among us in the humble forms of bread and wine and we kneel down before his Majesty, which is visible only to the eyes of faith, then this joyful and grateful profession is the one thing that makes man really free and truly great: "Dieu seul est grand."

Because God alone is truly great, he desires that we men, created in his image, should become like him in greatness as well. Otto von Habsburg is a great man, for whom we can thank God. Jesus speaks in the parable of the talents (Lk 19:11–28) about human greatness: about the gifts entrusted to us by God and about good or even excellent trading with those gifts. One steward had a tenfold return on his investment of the money that had been given to him: a brilliant performance from a commercial point of view (Lk 19:16).

Otto von Habsburg had originally been destined for another path in life: that of the successor to the throne of a great empire, a State consisting of many peoples. Yet the rulers of that time no longer wanted Karl von Habsburg, his father, to remain as emperor and king in that empire. The empire fell apart, and the resulting States fell prey to the misanthropic ideologies of mass murderers. Only slowly and arduously are these peoples recovering from the horrors of the twentieth century, which Nadezhda Mandelstam has called "the century of the wolves".

From his parents Otto von Habsburg also received another assignment: from his father, Blessed Karl, and from his mother, who instilled in him a profound sense of unselfish service that takes responsibility as a matter of course.

Thus he did not become the ruler of a large kingdom, but he did what distinguishes a great ruler: he served totally and unconditionally. Spiritually he never left the land that denied him a homecoming for so long; he stood by it unreservedly in the most difficult times, defended it to the best of his ability, and helped many oppressed Austrians. He fought for its liberation and so that it might be spared a division of the sort that Germany underwent. And he magnanimously disregarded all the insults, because he was concerned, never about himself, but rather about his "beloved Austria". For that we can thank him from our hearts in God's sight.

Yet it was never Austria alone that was his concern; but rather, his concern was for that common living space for which the House of Habsburg, the *Casa d'Austria*, stood for centuries. In his concern for and passionate interest in Europe, its peoples, and its relations to other peoples and continents, what was once said of his great ancestor, Emperor Karl V (d. 1558), about whom he wrote a biography, applies to him also: "In his kingdom the sun never sets."

His kingdom is his passion for the political, societal, and spiritual welfare of peoples. This kingdom knows no boundaries, because humaneness can know no boundaries. It is especially his commitment to Europe, however, for which we have to thank the Giver of all gifts and talents. The monarchy has fallen apart. Otto von Habsburg has become an architect of a new Europe, in which the old destructive forces of ideologies and nationalisms could be overcome. *Could*, because this victory is not yet assured, and it will be and remain so only if many leaders, following his example, set aside self-interest, partisanship, and short-term successes at the expense of others. That, of course, is possible only from a stance of strong faith and total dedication to service, as we see these qualities in Otto von Habsburg.

God alone is great. Yet he grants it to us occasionally to get a glimpse of his greatness in truly great men. For that we give thanks.

The Bridge Builder

Homily at the Requiem Mass
for Franz Cardinal König

On June 17, 1956, the new Viennese Archbishop Franz König said at the end of his first sermon in Saint Stephen's, "The festive splendor of the first entrance procession did not keep me from imagining also my final departure as a dead man, when I shall then have to render an accounting of my stewardship."

Since then almost fifty years have passed, filled with work to the very last. Today we accompany his mortal remains on their final journey to their interment in the bishops' crypt in the cathedral. We pray for the deceased, that God may accept his final accounting graciously and grant him eternal life in our heavenly homeland.

Living in the present

There have been many obituaries for Cardinal König, many moving, very personal testimonies by people from all walks of life in our country and all over the world. To these obituaries I do not want to add another one here. It is

March 27, 2004, Saint Stephen's Cathedral, Vienna. The Eucharist was celebrated by Cardinal Joseph Ratzinger as the Legate of Pope John Paul II. Franz Cardinal König was Archbishop of Vienna from 1956 to 1985.

appropriate instead to look forward. I think that that is just as Cardinal König would have wanted it.

I have never met a person advanced in years who lived so much in the present, in the present moment, as Cardinal König. Indeed, he could have related many things from his long life story, and he did so when asked about the past, without dwelling too much on it. His interest was in today and tomorrow.

Until the final hours of his earthly life Cardinal König was completely alert and attentive to the present, to people about whom he cared and asked, to things that were happening in the Church and the world.

That is why I am focusing my attention today on what his legacy means for us as a task. In recent days much has been said about the bridge builder. Bridges that span a wide river need piers that are firmly anchored in the current. Cardinal König's openness and his daring efforts at bridge building were supported by such solid piers. He was like the man in the Gospel about whom Jesus said that he had built his house on the rock. No storm, no flood could shake it (Mt 7:24–25).

When one faces death, the supporting foundations of one's life come to light. Cardinal König never made a show of his piety. It was simple and deep. Annemarie Fenzl, who accompanied him and cared for him until his final hour, writes, "As the days became more difficult, it became increasingly clear what the source of the Cardinal's strength was. After one Mass [which was celebrated in his room by a young priest], he said, 'That is what I live on!'"

The wideness of his heart, the openness of his mind, his lively interest in everything that affects people, came out of his profound, sincere union with God.

The first and most important legacy of Cardinal König, and subsequent task for us, is in my view attention to the solid foundation of the faith. The great bridge-builder Cardinal demonstrated for us that a faith anchored in Jesus Christ makes the heart wide and the mind open. "For me it is important to be committed to the truth, to God's Word, but combined with the power and strength of love for people", said Cardinal König in explaining his episcopal motto, "Veritatem facientes in caritate"—"Doing the truth in love".

Bridge-building efforts

So I should point out in particular three efforts at bridge building that I see as a legacy and a task, from the perspective of the firm pillar of faith.

1. The first legacy is his bridge-building effort of ecumenism. The many representatives of other Christian churches who are present here today testify to how stable the bridges built by Cardinal König are. Difficulties never discouraged him. We will continue along this path, true to Cardinal König's motto. His openness toward other Christians and other religions was always supported by his imperturbable true love for the Church, which never wavered, even in difficult hours.

2. The second legacy is his societal bridge-building effort. He, who had experienced the sorrowful period between the two world wars, knew how precious the bridges between the social forces in our country are. The task that his legacy leaves to us is not simply to "get along!", but rather the difficult but necessary demand to place what unites us above what separates us, to place the common good above special interests. Cardinal König set an example of this, not only for social dialogue in Austria, but also at the European level. The many visitors from neighboring countries who are here to celebrate and mourn with us testify to this.

3. His third legacy, which is now a task for us, occupied him intensively until his last days: the comprehensive protection of human life. His last great socio-political involvement was on behalf of humane care for the dying in Austria. As late as January 16, 2004, he wrote a moving letter to the President of the Austrian Constitutional Convention: "As a citizen of this country I am proud that in Austria there is a broad political consensus, transcending all party boundaries: People should die with another person on hand, and not at the hands of another person." And I quote again from this letter: "I view the idea of hospice in this context. Beyond the limits of medicine, it once again puts the person first." That is why Cardinal König asks the Constitutional Convention, "Euthanasia should be forbidden constitutionally in Austria in the future as well—as a sign of our commitment to a 'culture of life' and as a wake-up call for Europe."

May these words be for our country a testament and a commission. And these words, too, which Cardinal König spoke more than thirty years ago to the Executive Committee of the Austrian Federation of Trade Unions during the debate over protecting unborn human life: "I ask you to consider this: no man has the right to dispose of the life of another man, no matter what that life looks like; if this principle ever fails, then nothing will be left to protect man from being completely disposable. . . . Then they can do anything they want with us."

This, too, is a task for us who today are mourning this friend of life and praying for him.

My last look is toward the Mother of God, Our Lady of Mariazell, whom Cardinal König loved so much. Looking ahead to the great "Pilgrimage of Peoples", the conclusion of the Central European Catholic Conference on May 22, 2004, Cardinal König wrote at the beginning of that year:

"God willing, in May I will be there in Mariazell, too, with great joy and gratitude, conscious of my joint responsibility as former Archbishop of Vienna and as someone who shared the tragic experience of a Europe destroyed by war and hatred. I am also firmly convinced that Mariazell will solve all of the attendant organizational problems. Joy over such a completely new and hope-filled sort of encounter, transcending boundaries that not long ago still seemed insuperable, will overcome all difficulties."

God willed otherwise. Dear Cardinal König: You were no longer with us in Mariazell. Someone who is with God is with men also. You went home to God over the narrow bridge of death. I trust that you are still a bridge builder now and that "on the other side" you are a good intercessor for us with God. And when our final hour comes, help us, so that with God's help we, too, may succeed in this most important bridge-building effort, which leads beyond death to the shore of eternal life.

Where Do I Come from?
Where Am I Going?
What Is the Meaning of Life?

Homily at the Funeral Mass
for Thomas Klestil

"Fear not death's decree for you; remember, it embraces those before you and those after" (Sir 41:3, New American Bible). So a wise man from ancient Israel tells us: Ben Sira, or Jesus Sirach, as he is also called.

Yes, it happens to all of us. It is certain for everyone, and yet we usually ignore this certainty as we go about our daily routine. Death is one of the biggest taboos in our taboo-free age. Yet when death enters into our life, it brings with it all the essential questions for which we usually have no time in the whirl of our everyday activities. Again and again Cardinal König called to mind these fundamental questions of man: "Where do I come from? Where am I going? What is the meaning of my life?" Death sets things in proper order. Noisy and importunate questions recede, and the essential questions take on their importance.

July 10, 2004, Saint Stephen's Cathedral, Vienna. The homily refers to the following passages from the Bible: Sir 41:3–4, 11; Jn 12:23–26. Thomas Klestil was President of the Republic of Austria from 1992 to 2004. He died unexpectedly a few days before the end of his second term in office.

Where do I come from?

Allow me, dear friend, to say a personal word to you in this hour: Although death separates us externally, our common faith tells us that we are united even beyond death, more deeply than before, because we are united in God and through God. Indeed, you have not become a shadow, have not dissolved into nothingness. You live; that is our firm belief. You have gone before us to the place where death will one day lead us all, hopefully all of us to a happy destination. We should practice solidarity also by helping one another not to miss the eternal destination of our earthly journey.

"Where do I come from?" You never denied the "modest circumstances", as they say, from which you came. You never forgot the deep faith of your mother. It accompanied you especially in the difficult hours. It is consoling to believe that you have found her again at the destination in which she so firmly believed.

The parish staffed by the Salesian Fathers of Don Bosco in Vienna-Erdberg made a strong impression on your youth. You gladly and gratefully remembered that. One of the youngsters then, Ludwig Schwarz, is a bishop today.

You had the privilege of pursuing a successful diplomatic career. How important are the people who unselfishly support us along such a path! Federal Chancellor Josef Klaus (d. 2001) was such a man. And how important it is to show gratitude toward those people! Forgetting to do so is a terrible thing.

Much has been said about the services you performed as a diplomat and a head of state. Certainly today, when so many individuals with the most important responsibilities have come from all over the world to pay you their last respects, our country realizes how much you did for us, how high their esteem for you was and is. You were in exemplary fashion a genuine citizen of the world. The guests from all over the world provide evidence of this to you and to us. You were a European out of the deepest conviction. You made a substantial contribution toward bringing Austria into the European Union. You were unceasingly active in accompanying and helping our friendly neighbors in Central and Eastern Europe on their path to integration [into the EU]. The presence of so many high-ranking representatives from those countries is an expression of thanks for that. Finally, you were a passionate Austrian patriot and wanted, as you yourself used to say, to let no one surpass you in your love for Austria. It is painful and humiliating for us to observe that you, too, met with the typically Austrian fate of receiving only after death the recognition that had long since been accorded to you elsewhere. All the more reason that you should have today and henceforth the thanks of Austria, our thanks.

Where am I going?

Your office placed you so completely in the public eye that there was hardly any private sphere left. This became evident at the time of your severe illnesses, but especially in your difficulties with marriage and family. Many people in our country took an interest in this, and the fact that it touched and moved so many is a clear sign that this area is essential in our life.

With most people you shared a deep yearning for a happy marriage and family harmony. Like so many people today, you went through the painful and difficult experience of breaking up a relationship and beginning a new one, with all of this made even more difficult by the magnifying glass of publicity.

It is not up to us to judge. Jesus said this emphatically: "Judge not, that you be not judged" (Mt 7:1). May we never forget these words of Jesus. With dismay we see how great a longing there is today for successful relationships, a longing for security in marriage and family, and how difficult it has become. You respected the Church's position in this question, even when it was not easy for you. It is not easy for the Church, either, to find the middle way between the absolutely necessary defense of marriage and the family, on the one hand, and the equally necessary mercy to be shown to human failure and new beginnings, on the other. Perhaps, dear friend, your death is an incentive for us all to make a common effort on behalf of both, in the knowledge that both are necessary and that neither is simple.

What is the meaning of my life?

Where are you now? Where are the dead? Your dead body is here. But where are you? We cannot imagine it, but we can believe it. We firmly believe that you are home, at home with God. And we believe that there is no greater happiness. Jesus compares death with the grain of wheat that falls to the ground and dies; it dies so as to bear much fruit.

"What is the meaning of my life?" What, if not "to bear much fruit"? That requires, as Jesus says, losing one's life (cf. Jn 12:24–25). You deployed your life completely; you did not spare yourself, to the last, for the sake of our country and its people and those far beyond it. For that you have our heartfelt thanks.

You loved the shrine of Mariazell very much and did much for it and entrusted yourself from childhood to Mary's protection. And so I will do that also for you, together with all who want to join in:

Holy Mary, Mother of God,
pray for us sinners,
now and at the hour of our death.
Amen.

Reconciliation Takes Precedence over Everything

Homily at the Requiem Mass for Kurt Waldheim

"Make friends quickly with your accuser, while you are going with him to court" (Mt 5:25). Jesus' words stand before us here today as a serious challenge, as a word that it is not easy to get past. In his "last word" the deceased asks all those who opposed him critically to reflect again on their motives "and to grant me—if possible—a belated reconciliation". And he adds the moving words, "Perhaps this, too, has become easier through my departure from this earth."

Reconciliation takes precedence over everything. Even ministering at the altar comes afterward. Be reconciled before you enter into the presence of God. This matter of reconciliation has high priority. The language that Jesus uses in the Sermon on the Mount, from which today's Gospel reading is taken, is surprisingly stern. We find here, not the loving, understanding, all-forgiving traits that predominate in our picture of God today, but rather clear words that, indeed, sound unmerciful: "Every one who is angry with

June 23, 2007, Saint Stephen's Cathedral, Vienna. The homily refers to the following passages from the Bible: Eph 4:29—5:2; Mt 5:21–26. Kurt Waldheim was General Secretary of the United Nations from 1972 to 1981 and President of the Republic of Austria from 1986 to 1992.

his brother shall be liable to judgment.... And whoever says, 'You fool!' shall be liable to the hell of fire" (Mt 5:22). The Torah, the Divine Law, forbids not only murder but anger itself, judgmental words, contemptuous speech about another. Reconciliation is absolutely necessary, as is evident from the weight of the sanctions imposed by Jesus on the irreconcilable: judgment, punishment—indeed, hellfire! In my opinion we need the clarity of this language. For scarcely anything is so bitterly hard for us as reconciliation.

Before us lies a man in his transitoriness, who marvelously, powerfully symbolizes this for us: at the end of his life he asked in an almost unprecedented fashion for forgiveness. Why was he seeking reconciliation? No longer so as to make his own life easier. No longer because he himself could expect something from it. No longer to beg for approval, sympathy, or praise, but rather out of a need—as he was on his way to meet his judge—to comply with the most profound precept of a Christian life.

He did not combine his offer of reconciliation—no, his request for reconciliation—with the things that might seem natural to us: with a final attack on those who think differently or with attempts to exonerate himself personally. We can sense in his "last word" a deep knowledge about what could make our world brighter: unconditional, disinterested reconciliation.

Can we manage that? Is not this demand of the Gospel exorbitant? Did Kurt Waldheim succeed at it? What does a look at his journey tell us? Two characteristics stand out that made his life prominent but also burdened it.

Living in the high-voltage area

On the one hand, there is the great span of his life, through all the lights and shadows of eighty-nine years and then some. As he himself wrote at the end of his life, he had to extend the arc of his life, from war to peace, from dictatorship to freedom, from poverty to prosperity, farther than a man usually accommodates under the arc of his destiny.

And then there is the enormous high-voltage area occupied by the interests and hopes of so many peoples, nations, interest groups, and also the tensions between the opposing sides of so many conflicts, in which the deceased was exposed to criticism and challenged to a degree that almost no other son of this land has ever experienced. To live in the midst of these contradictions and oppositions and to fight for justice, reconciliation, and peace—all this makes one vulnerable and leaves wounds in its wake. No one lives more dangerously than the mediator, the conciliator, the man who seeks peace.

I think that no one—not even his most passionate critics—will dispute that the deceased, after his experiences of dictatorship and war, death and misery, staked his whole life on reconciliation. In his career decision, in his decades-long service on behalf of Austria and the community of nations—and well into old age. He recognized sooner than others that peace and justice, justice and brotherhood are inseparable.

It may be that he tried to reconcile, to unite, and to exclude what is burdensome perhaps even in areas where irreconcilables stand in opposition and must be called irreconcilable as well. Out of this passion much sorrow developed, which overshadowed his life.

Kurt Waldheim stood, with his own life and his task as a seeker of peace, like almost no other at the crossroads of a fundamental human and political question: the question of how much forgetting and how much mindfulness man needs. At the end of his tragic journey, King Lear says to his daughter Cordelia, whom he has found once again, "Pray you

now, forget and forgive." Does it really take both? I think
so, but in the proper measure. If we were to remember all
the evil that weighs on our history, we could not live. That
is why many peace treaties in the past enjoined the com-
batants as a duty to forget all the horrors.

But the reverse is also true: If we were to forget everything that was wrong and wicked, we would not be men.
We could reflect on nothing and learn nothing. We would
have no past and therefore no future.

The measure of reconciliation

Therefore it is a question of the proper measure. We must
forget what divides us—and be mindful of what brings us
forward. Reconciliation cannot be commanded of anyone.
It must not be forced externally but, rather, must come
from within. And it needs the space afforded by grace, or
else reconciliation cannot succeed. The Apostle Paul writes
in the Letter to the Ephesians, "Be kind to one another,
tenderhearted, forgiving one another, as God in Christ
forgave you" (Eph 4:32). Because we have already been forgiven, we can forgive. Because we have in faith the incomparably consoling and strengthening certainty that we are
God's "beloved children", as Paul says (Eph 5:1), we can
also confidently entrust to him our failure and confess our
guilt.

How often in recent years I heard the deceased say, "I
could not have endured it all without faith." To have faith,
however, means to trust, to know that we are safe and secure
with the One who, as Paul tells us, "loved us and gave
himself for us" (cf. Gal 2:20).

Should not our rule for dealing with one another be,
"As *God* has done for me, so I do for you"? As God accepts
me, so I will try to be tolerant of others. In our merciless,

incriminating society, it is so difficult to speak honestly about guilt and failure because the necessary space of goodwill is lacking, without which self-justification becomes a compulsive survival skill. How liberating, then, are the faith-filled words of the deceased: "In the face of death, all the divisions in life are resolved. Good and evil, light and shadow, merits and mistakes stand now before a Judge who alone knows the truth. I go into his presence consoled—knowing that he is just and gracious."

He will now experience his grace; it will hide and shelter him after all the beauty and bitterness in his life. That is what we pray for in this hour. We pray also for his widow. For more than half a century they were an exemplary married couple, a family that supported each other. Without the grace of that happy marriage, the burden of his offices, even more than the burden of unjust accusations, would have been unbearable. It was a beautiful sign of God's grace that Kurt Waldheim was able to die surrounded by his beloved family.

Thus at the end of the earthly pilgrimage of our former President of the Republic there is, above all, gratitude. "Led by God, I depart from this life with much gratitude"—so begins his "final word". In that life, that eternal life in which he believed, to which he has now gone home reconciled and in peace, he will not forget us or his "much-beloved Austria" or the many peoples of the world and their needs and cares.

To us, however, who are still on our pilgrim way, applies the urgent word of Jesus: "Make friends quickly with your accuser, while you are going with him to court." There is still time!

IV

REMEMBERING THE TERROR

Mauthausen

Remembering and Reflecting

We hold our breath. In Mauthausen, for almost seven years, evil was at home. A bit of hell on earth. Here people from all over Europe suffered and died: Jews and Christians, Romanies and other gypsies, Jehovah's Witnesses and homosexuals, the handicapped and political dissenters.

Austrians were among the victims—and among the perpetrators. We have to live with this simultaneity of sorrow and shame, incalculable suffering and unbounded brutality. The concentration camps in our homeland, in Mauthausen and Gusen, in Hartheim, Sankt Radegund and elsewhere, press us hard with immediate questions we would much rather discuss at a safe distance.

And they confront us with the indivisibility of our past. Everything that has happened in this country, the good as well as the terrible, remains inscribed forever in our history. We must acknowledge both, if the future is not to become a repetition of history.

But Mauthausen, with its wide network of outlying camps, has yet another terrifying experience in store for us who were born afterward. Back then the devastation here was not brought on by some criminal gangs from a far-off land, not by beasts, not by raving fanatics from another culture, with another religion, of another civilization.

May 8, 2005, commemorative address, Mauthausen.

No, they were people like us. They had wives and children at home whom they loved, dreams and yearnings like ours, their Christmas tree, and Schiller and Goethe on the bookshelf. Perpetrators and victims could not be distinguished by the color of their skin or by their facial features.

The front line between good and evil in those days ran through the middle of our people, through families, indeed, often through the middle of one's own heart. Every one of us might have been either one: a victim, but also a perpetrator. Nothing tells us with definitive assurance on which side we would have stood then or would be standing today.

The significance of remembering

In the Gospel of Matthew there is a frightening saying of Jesus: "Woe to you, scribes and Pharisees, hypocrites! For you ... adorn the monuments of the righteous, saying, 'If we had lived in the days of our fathers, we would not have taken part with them in shedding the blood of the prophets'" (Mt 23:29–30).

This is what compels us again and again to remember: the admission of our weakness and of our susceptibility to temptation. When things get serious, there are only a few very small steps that separate us from confusion and mixed emotions, from enticement and involvement.

But then, too, there is our knowledge of the power of evil—and of the depth of God-forsakenness. Tomorrow or the day after tomorrow it may again come along, clothed in a new ideology, with new persuasive power.

And not for the first time, but in a state of shock unprecedented before the Holocaust, we men are faced with the question from the Book of Job: "Where were you, God?" Where were you when women and children, able-bodied men and the elderly were sent into the murderous slavery of National Socialism and into the death chambers? To such questions there are no simple answers that can really convince our human thinking.

The lament over God's absence is also a lament over the absence of man. Where was man, where was mankind, when such terrible things were being inflicted on our brothers and sisters? We could and ought to find an answer to that question at least, especially since the core of the Christian faith says that God has sided with the tormented and the oppressed. The Word spoken from the Cross tells us: That is where he is to be found.

All the more reason to ask: How could all this happen in a thoroughly Christian country in which the Cross of Christ is omnipresent? Even though among the victims of the National Socialist terror there were many who suffered and were killed for their Christian faith, we must still acknowledge how much guilt Christians, too, brought upon themselves by their many failures.

Day after day we experience how fragile all human certainties can be, the safeguards that protect us against intolerance, injustice, indeed, outright violence. We experience how difficult it is to accept what has happened and to live in the truth without ifs, ands, or buts. We recognize how brittle our solidarity is; how quickly we feel threatened by the thought of old enemies, and how laborious it is to build and maintain lasting bridges of trust and mutual respect.

What, then, is the significance of remembering? And why should places like Mauthausen emerge forever from the stream of forgetfulness like a rock that the rapid river of time cannot carry away? The history of the last century is a powerful alarm, thwarting any attempt to smooth over or cover up history.

Adolf Hitler himself offered terrible testimony to this when he dismissed the last doubts about his campaign to annihilate the Jews and the Slavic peoples with the words, "Who today still remembers the Armenians?" And indeed, the Armenian tragedy of 1915 remained concealed so long by silence and the failure to remember that subsequent dictators learned from it the lesson that the expulsion and annihilation of entire peoples is in fact possible and feasible. Even in the twentieth century. Mauthausen is horrific proof of it.

Sixty years have passed since the liberation from the National Socialist dictatorship. Not one of us would consider the accomplishments of recent decades insignificant: the gradual unification of Europe, the triumphant march of freedom and democracy, the globalization of communications and of human rights. And yet we sense that the battle against the darkness of yesterday was never won. That the way out of danger is still a long one. It is much more immediate than we suspect: it leads through our everyday routine.

Signs of hope in the fight against the darkness

But where are the handholds, the signs of hope that are so necessary in the battle against the darkness of those days?

The first sign of hope consists in *listening to our conscience*, to that interior voice. To the eternal law of the dignity, indeed, the divine likeness of every person, which is inscribed on our hearts.

Next comes *attentiveness to our thoughts and actions*. World history does not take place somewhere far away from us and is not shaped by distant, foreign, and anonymous forces. We are all a responsible part of history. Every day, with every deed, with every word, with every omission. The rough draft of the future is being written by us today.

The third handhold is *remembering* our own mistakes, but even more—God's faithfulness. The God of Israel, whom we also invoke as Father, does not tire of calling to us through his prophets: "Do not forget a single one of my deeds, do not forget my history with you. You must remain rooted in it." In this sense our remembering is always a sort of fidelity to God also, who forgets nothing, for whom nothing is lost and nothing forgotten: no tear, no suffering, but also not the quiet, hidden goodness that existed in the midst of the horror and always will exist.

The last two petitions of the Our Father are: "And lead us not into temptation, but deliver us from evil."

> God grant that we, the people of today, may never get into situations in which we fail out of weakness, cowardice, or fear and betray mankind.

> God grant that the evil that came to an end in 1945 may never return.

> *Deliver us from the power of the Evil One. Grant that the whole human family will one day, soon, be freed from his power.*

The People of Israel Live

Austria's Bishops in Yad Vashem

It is difficult to rise to speak in this place, where every word really ought to become mute. And yet speaking about what happened is, again and again, perhaps the most important service we can perform to keep from forgetting. Eli Wiesel once said, "If anything at all will save mankind, then it is remembering."

We remember here the immeasurable suffering of the Jewish people. We remember many questions that dismay us in particular as Austrian bishops. We are here as bishops of a country in which one Adolf Hitler learned his insane ideas. We stand here in great perplexity and ask ourselves what there was in the history of our country, in the heads and hearts of the people of our country, that made such monstrosities of evil possible. And we wonder why God allowed such a thing: "Where were you, God? Where were you, when women and children, old and young people were sent to the death chambers?"

And although we know there is no conclusive answer, we know one thing for certain: logically and ultimately these questions are addressed to us: "Where was man and where was mankind when our brothers and sisters were afflicted so terribly? And where was God among us?" We

November 8, 2007, speech at the memorial Yad Vashem, Jerusalem.

remember in this place a time when God was extremely distant and the hellish depths to which a world without God can plummet.

We remember the word of the Prophet Isaiah: "I will give in my house and within my walls a monument and a name ... ; I will give them an everlasting name which shall not be cut off" (Is 56:5). Even though the ashes of countless tormented, degraded, murdered people were scattered to the winds and no stone is left to tell of them, nothing is lost and nothing is forgotten in God's sight, not one tear, not one sorrow. But also not the great deal of quiet, hidden goodness that existed in the midst of the horror and that will always exist.

The "Avenue of the Righteous among the Nations" by which we arrived here reminds us in the midst of an ocean of failure and guilt about a light of hope. This Avenue tells us: Even in the darkness of the Shoah, there were people, Christians too, who opposed that brutality. Of course, even though quite a few Austrian names are recorded along this Avenue, there were too few of them, too few righteous persons.

It is no accident that we stand here, on the eve of the commemoration of the November pogroms of the year 1938 in Yad Vashem, in mourning, consternation, and shame over the full extent of what had already become evident during that terrible night of murder and arson and that then—also because of human weakness, cowardice, and fear—was able to grow beyond all bounds.

In this connection the history of our Austrian homeland, and with it also the history of the Catholic Church in our country, is a mixture of enormous guilt and yet of courage and resistance also. Blessed Franz Jägerstätter (d. 1943) and those like him were, as we know, lonely beacons and remained so even long after the dictatorship collapsed. The expression "We were just doing our duty" was unequivo-cally unmasked by someone like Franz Jägerstätter as being just not enough.

In the Gospel of the Apostle Matthew there is a fright-ening saying of Jesus: "Woe to you . . . , hypocrites! For you . . . adorn the monuments of the righteous, saying, 'If we had lived in the days of our fathers, we would not have taken part with them in shedding the blood of the proph-ets'" (Mt 23:29–30). This is what always compels us to remember: the admission of our weakness and of our sus-ceptibility to temptation.

When we visited the "Children's Memorial", dedicated to the one and a half million murdered Jewish children, we experienced in an almost indescribable way sorrow and hor-ror, but also, as contradictory as it may seem, joy and grat-itude. A starry heaven of infinity was extinguished at the hands of criminals, and yet not consigned forever to dark-ness and the power of evil. We came out of the darkness of the memorial into the bright daylight again. At the end of this memorial, there is a view of Jerusalem. We believe as Christians with our elder brothers and sisters in the resur-rection. We believe that no crime will have the last word, nor will death. For the criminal dream of extinguishing the people of the First Covenant was not realized: *am Israël ha*, the people of Israel live.

V

LITERATURE

"But there will be grace then, too"

The Works of Gertrud von Le Fort

It is amazing how quickly literary critics have become silent about the works of Gertrud von Le Fort (d. 1971). The author of *Hymns to the Church*, who was greeted by Paul Claudel (d. 1955) as a great hope, seems no longer to be on the "curriculum" of German instruction today. We can hardly expect that Le Fort's novels and short stories would meet today with the same response as in her time. Has the author, then, already had her day? Can her works still be read as anything other than "materials for the history of literature"? The author unquestionably no longer has the large public that she had in the first and even the second decade after the war. It is certainly not easy to pin down the reasons for this rapid "alienation".

Much of it may be due to the author's style, the *faux*-historical tone of many of her stories, a certain linguistic mannerism—although all this is to be found in works by other authors who have remained quite popular (I am thinking, for instance, of the novel *Der Erwählte* by Thomas

On the occasion of the one hundredth birthday of Gertrud von Le Fort. First published in *Internationale Katholische Zeitschrift Communio* 6 (1976): 548–55.

Her works are cited using the following abbreviations: E: *Die Erzählungen* (Munich, 1968); HK: *Hymnen an die Kirche* (Munich, 1924); HL: *Hälfte des Lebens: Erinnerungen* (Munich, 1965); WG: *"Woran ich glaube" und andere Aufsätze* (Zurich, 1968).

Mann, d. 1955). The heavy cargo of theological thinking may sometimes impede the narrative mobility, so that occasionally the reader has the impression that the author is basically illustrating a religious idea. Yet there are plenty of examples of "top-heavy" literature that are very much in vogue (for example, Bertold Brecht, d. 1956). Whatever the reasons for the swift decrease of Gertrud von Le Fort's literary popularity may be, it is not our intention here to inquire into the literary validity of her works or the chances that they will survive in the publishing world. Claudel was convinced that this was a literary *oeuvre* that would last. Only the future can tell whether he was right. Now we are probably still too close to the time and the intellectual space in which Gertrud von Le Fort lived and her work breathed.

I suspect that this is the main problem with reading Le Fort today. We do not yet have the necessary distance, not so much from the person of the author as from the recent past and its wounds. Gertrud von Le Fort is too bound up with her world; she adhered to her "profession of faith in a truly holy Germany" (Erich Przywara, d. 1972) with a candor and an ideological insouciance that may seem too direct and almost painful for many readers. Perhaps the rediscovery of this author will be reserved for a future generation unburdened by the traumas of the past. The writer of these lines belongs to a generation for which the world of Gertrud von Le Fort is already history. The attempt in the following pages to inquire into the family background of the author and her intellectual world is not a "nostalgic" look back at the past combined with a lamentation over present conditions. It is instead a question that, aside from all literary evaluation, is directed toward a *person* who intensely experienced the upheavals of her time and sensed that they heralded even greater ones. It is a matter of asking a great Christian for instruction about what is yet to come, our appreciation of Gertrud von Le Fort's prophetic significance.

Background

Her family background makes it difficult to accredit her work according to the widely accepted criteria of German studies. The "socio-economic basis" and way of life of the Prussian landed aristocracy, her "late-bourgeois education"— all that is not exactly apt to assure her a place in the "basic guidelines" for literary studies. Of course, Gertrud von Le Fort, for her part, did little to prevent this problem. Her novels and short stories deal almost nonchalantly with the world in which she grew up. "Die Unschuldigen" [The innocent] (1953), "Am Tor des Himmels" [At heaven's gate] (1954), and "Das fremde Kind" [The strange child] (1961) evoke a declining world: the rural, "feudal" life at a castle. Although the author is in no way ashamed of her background and does not deny it, neither does she idealize "everything that is past". "It was not being 'unsocial', as some later maintained, that caused our former world to fail; it was just that it had outlived its time—why, I do not know. It is a mystery of world events, why something perfect in itself should become outmoded. What was destined to fall then was not wrong, but it had exhausted its possibilities" (E 569).

"Writing is not a work alongside of living, but rather a form of living" (E 151). The question about the meaning of transience, or perhaps even more about what proves to be lasting and salvific in all things that pass away, the question about the great "mystery of world events" is posed for the writer by the circumstances of her life. Her work of writing is a search for the possible answer. One of her characters says on one occasion, "I belong right down the line

to a sacrificed generation—one that has been called to death"
(E 160). Gertrud von Le Fort's works express the belief
that the sacrifice of that generation, the massive slaughter
of innocent life ultimately was not in vain. I am convinced
that this creative center elevates the writer's work, if not to
the level of a timeless classic, at least to the status of the
prophetically valid, so that it has today an urgent and liberating relevance.

Life that has been called to death—if that is supposed to
be the center of history, then is it not the tragic view of
history that Reinhold Schneider (d. 1958) affirmed? In
gloomy retrospect (*Verhüllter Tag*), he views his life and that
of countless contemporaries as being swept along into the
tragedy of inevitable downfalls. In his literary work he strug-
gles "to cope with downfall". Behind all the collapses of
history and of the present day he glimpses an "insolubly
tragic situation" (178): "I hear nothing other than an inex-
pressible, tragic melody." What unfolds here is no longer
just the inevitable conflict of history; it is a tragedy that
runs deeper, down to the very roots of being: "Now again,
becoming more isolated, I drew near to the landscape of
my youth: a rocky valley from which I see no exit, the
'dark place' in which an incurable pain is buried. This pain
is not Providence or consequence, but rather essence" (213).

What governs in the tragedy of downfalls is ultimately
not historical drama but rather an eternal drama (220), behind
and beyond all time: the tragedy is in God himself, if indeed
"contradiction is characteristic of all that is divine", the two
faces of light and darkness, "Grantor of blessings and
Destroyer" (224). Of course, if that is the case, then the
drama of human history is reduced to a mere reflection of
the eternal drama, which one must recognize and endure.
Here Reinhold Schneider's retrospective inquiry into the
meaning of all the downfalls comes close to the Gnostic

solution (80 f.). There must be education for the "impossible-necessary" character of life: "How could the school have equipped people for an era of collapses—and that was its task—when its own foundations were giving way? ... If the locus of our life is history, with the immense responsibility of that name, then there is nothing left but to prepare youth for the tragic, incurable character of historical life. For in history necessary demands appear that necessarily remain unfulfilled" (37f.).

One cannot sum up and contrast the different paths in life followed by Reinhold Schneider and Gertrud von Le Fort. And the question remains whether the author of *Philipp II.* and *Innozenz III.* did not fall short of the demands made by his own literary *oeuvre*. The only thing that matters is how this "coping with downfall" is attempted. It is no accident that the Reinhold Schneider of the later period finds the last possible expression of his "existential mood" (216) in the "Protestant form" (89) of Christianity, in Martin Luther's lonely experience of the "coincidence of being destroyed and being saved" (70, 212).

Gertrud von Le Fort hears the answer about the meaning of all the downfalls, not in an "ineffably tragic melody", but rather in the "voice of the Bride". The unmistakably personal sound of this voice is probably what moves the reader of her writings and does not let go, from the *Hymns to the Church* to her last short story, "Der Dom" [The cathedral], in which the homelike character of the Church is viewed once more with refined, childlike clarity. I think that there are few figures of our time who have seen with such prophetic urgency in the mystery of the Church the center of the historical upheavals. In light of this mystery, Gertrud von Le Fort coped with the fragmentation, destruction, and hatred of her time—no, more precisely, we would have to say that she thoroughly loved it. For about the Church and about her alone in human history one can say that "There is no hour to end your hour, and your boundaries are unbounded, for you carry within your bosom the mercy of the Lord!" (HK 21).

Gertrud von Le Fort definitely acknowledged her belief in the triumph of mercy—and there is only one mercy, for even "the world's mercy is your runaway daughter" (HK 22). "I believe in God's love, I believe in man, even in the atomic age I believe in the triumph of mercy" (WG 67). This is not a naïve belief in progress. The author of *The Eternal Woman* constantly pointed out the danger that man, and especially woman, might acquire a "mechanical heart", whereby in their desire for technological control they imperceptibly become the ones being controlled. Yet this very defeat of humanity becomes an opening for grace. The author sees the meaning of the Marian dogmas in the fact that "the image of those who are painfully subjected" (39) shows the way that can "help even our technological age break through to a humane age" (40). "Belief in the creative forces of our time also" (118) is not a matter of trite optimism but, rather, faith in the reality of the Church and of the Divine Mercy that she carries in her bosom. In this faith she can even say, "When a world is going under, that means we must not look back" (128).

The assurance with which Gertrud von Le Fort expresses this faith in her works may well be another difficulty that makes the author less accessible today. Certainty is unwelcome; a definite faith is suspected of prematurely terminating the seeker's question, the risk of faith. This suspicion can arise only when seeking is preferred to finding, when the certainty of faith is rejected as unbelief: "You are like a road that never arrives" (HK 18). Surely, the clear certainty of Gertrud von Le Fort was preceded by a long search, at the end of which is, of course, the voice of the Church: "You say to those who doubt, 'Be silent', and to those who question, 'Kneel down!' You say to the fugitives, 'Surrender', and to those on the wing, 'Let yourselves fall down!'" (HK 13). Only about the Church can one say, "and every pilgrimage finds a home in you" (HK 13).

Heritage

The author never surrendered her personal life to the curious public. These "sheltered sources" of her literary work are mentioned in only a few reticent memoirs (*Hälfte des Lebens*), which surely are intended, not as an autobiography,[1] but rather as "a quiet accounting" (HL 6).

Almost no shadows fell on her childhood and youth, which were "filled with the final glow of a declining epoch" (40), "which, however, we children, naturally, and probably our parents, too, did not realize at all" (15). When the writer remembers the world of her childhood and youth, the estate in Mecklenburg that they called home, the Rococo-style charm of the residence, Ludwigslust, and imperial Berlin, what is surprising, amid all the wistfulness, is the ease and the love with which she speaks about a Germany that to many seems impossible to love now, after all the horrors. And yet her entire literary *oeuvre* testifies to how profoundly Gertrud von Le Fort experienced the pain of its disappearance.

The writer was familiar with the temptation to take a tragic view of history, to be "irremediably pained" by it (R. Schneider). She speaks about the child's "enthusiasm for the manners of the old empire" (38), but also about her lasting sorrow over the Germany of her youth, about the "never-healed wound concerning the former empire, in

[1] "Woe to him who wants to be historical himself": E. Staiger, in *Gertrud von le Fort: Werk und Bedeutung:"Der Kranz der Engel" im Widerstreit der Meinungen* (Munich, 1950), 5.

whose decline I found myself, but which I have never for-gotten" (46). Nothing about this pain is denied, nor her "deep sorrow over world history" (92). In Rome she met with "the silent sublimity and tragedy of these moving ruins. From them I learned to bear the storms and jolts of the past without tears" (100).

The attitude of "Spiegelchen's" grandmother in *Schweiß-tuch der Veronika* [*The Veil of Veronica*] embodies this noble perseverance in the midst of transience. It appears in a more tragic, lacerated form in the professor at Heidelberg University in *Der Kranz der Engel* [The angel's crown], a character probably based on her teacher, Ernst Troeltsch (d. 1923), in whom she encountered "this melancholy insight" (100); what disturbs Gertrud von Le Fort about Ernst Troeltsch is that "mournful atmosphere of inescapable transiency",[2] the sense that there is "no way out" (HL 100). The temptation appears even more terrifyingly in the figure of Enzio, who follows it to its logical conclusion: destruction. His youth-ful enthusiasm at the imperial tribunals in Rome and in the emperor's tomb in Speyer becomes, after a humiliation from which he never recovers, a demolishing hatred for all that has been. The floodgates of the underworld are opened; faced with their power, the grandmother's noble humanity and the professor's tragic half-belief fail. "Enzio's tragedy is Germany's fall from poetry and spirituality, from creative writing and thinking, into 'work', into the movement for the revival of Germany as a power."[3]

The controversy unleashed by *Der Kranz der Engel* is to a great extent forgotten today. What remains valid is the attempt at a Christian answer to Germany's tragedy and, beyond that, to the power of evil. ("Evil has no other power

[2] Theodor Kampmann, in ibid., 50.
[3] A. Dempf, in ibid., 40.

than the powerlessness of good" [E 208].) The words written then by Theodor Kampmann are still true: "We consider ourselves obliged to point out this interpretation,
because it is the only one to appear in German-speaking
lands that really does justice to this great subject."[4] Unsolv-
able tragedy is not the last word about the German past, or
about history as a whole, but rather the word in the final
chorus of the *Grossen Zapfenstreichs* [a German military cer-
emonial], which holds a key position in the novel: "I pray
to the power of love" (HL 46).

By her own admission, something that her uncle wrote
to her shortly before the outbreak of National Socialism
was what lit the way for the writer through the cataclysmic
destruction, and she treasured it as a legacy: "I will no longer experience that era, but you will. *Do not forget that there
will still be grace even then*" (HL 65). Gertrud von Le Fort
made this statement the centerpiece of one of her most
gripping short stories: "Das fremde Kind" [The strange child].

Center

The period depicted in this late story (1961) spans the writer's lifetime. Much of it bears the stamp of personal remi-
niscence: the fading charms of the summerhouse in the
country, the sense that aristocratic life is coming to an end,
war and defeat, the rise of National Socialism and war again,
new and unimaginable guilt, the horrible murder of the
Jews. In the center stands the character "Gläschen" [Little
Glass], the embodiment of the defenseless fragility of mercy.
In "Gläschen" we see the only power that endures: "This
world's will to destroy is merely shattered against mercy and
against it alone", we read in a historical novella that seeks

---

[4] Theodor Kampmann, in ibid., 7.

an answer to the question of why tyranny is permitted ("Die Consolata", E 271).

Gläschen's "remarkably sensitive relation to everything that is alive" (E 555), which in the old, intact world appeared to be sympathetic sentimentality, was to appear in a new light with the manifestation of the terrible face of the will to power, with its contempt for life. Yet precisely in this contrast the power of mercy is proved. Gläschen's smiling tenderness, which "was almost always aroused by the defense-lessness and helplessness of creatures" (583), could certainly not stop at the ultimate helplessness of those who have fallen inextricably into the hands of the civil authorities, embod-ied in the character of Jeskow. As an S.S. officer, he becomes guilty of killing Jews: "I still see the little Jewish girl in front of me, beseeching me with her imploring eyes as they were taking her away" (601).

He encounters these eyes again in the Jewish girl whom Gläschen takes in and claims as her daughter when the girl's mother is sent to the concentration camp. "'How coura-geous you are, Gläschen', I said, deeply moved. She laughed unabashedly. 'Oh, no! I was not brave; it is just that I was not afraid'" (605). The eyes of this defenseless, affectionate child symbolize for Jeskow, a wounded man sent home from the front, the whole torment of his self-accusations, his guilt, for which "I can never forgive myself" (615). Only faith in the reality of vicarious grace is capable of easing that tor-ment. In this child, whom he must keep rescuing for the duration of the war, Jeskow is conquered by the power of mercy he had rejected in Gläschen. Consequently, how-ever, "the furies withdrew from him forever" (621). Ger-trud von Le Fort sees here the only possibility of genuinely "overcoming the past". On one occasion the uncle of the female narrator says to her, "My child, we cannot love our people only when it suits our vanity; we must love them just as God loves mankind, which continually disappoints him.... Certainly, the judgment will be terrible, *but there will still be grace, even then*" (596).

"To love Germany"—saying that today, without blushing or cynical scorn, and also without forgetting or repressing anything, is possible only by the path the writer shows us. "The world has not forgiven our people, and that is quite in order, although not particularly important. The only important thing is that our people has not forgiven itself and must not forgive itself: there is, however, a vicarious grace" (620f.).

The mystery of vicarious substitution is also central to the story that is dedicated to "the memory of the children who died in the World War": "Die Unschuldigen" [The innocent] (1953), in which the author takes as her theme the guilt for the massacre at Oradour. No blame is assigned. The sorrow is too great; the picture is too painful: the children burned in the French village church, the children gassed in the concentration camps, those killed by bombs, lying like dolls on the pavement, the children frozen as they fled across the lagoon: "The whole world, indeed, is full of the suffering of the innocent!" (351). After Oradour, after Auschwitz, after Dresden, can anyone still believe in the mercy of God? There is no pat answer. Yet her glance falls at Christmas upon the picture of that little Child "with scepter and throne, a very tiny Child with the imperial orb—how terribly distressing!" "Poor little Christ Child, have you ever been able to prevent something horrible?" (349). There is no solution, only consent to vicarious grace. In this, in the invisible reality of grace, meet the lonely surviving mother in Oradour and the German mother who accepts the death of her child as vicarious substitution: "Mary, take my child" (367).

Only the omnipotence of mercy can descend into the abyss of the dehumanization of this [twentieth] century. In

"Die Opferflamme" [The sacrificial flame] (1941), it says
about a Russian poet: "This poor man had evidently escaped
the demons of his homeland only externally; internally they
had caught up with him ..." (F 156); in him there was
"something completely void, completely hopeless" (154),
and the author senses, as she did in the case of Enzio's struggle with nihilism in *Der Kranz der Engel*, that this man can
no longer be reached by the faith that fills her (154). After
all he has lived through, there is nothing left for him to say
but: "Love has been abolished today all over the world"
(157). How can the eternal Love still reach this man? "If a
soul can no longer believe in God's grace, then man must
take over God's grace" (E 603). In this thought Gertrud
von Le Fort sees the answer. She derives from it no "struc-
tural law", no global formula. This answer is reserved to
faith. Such vicarious substitution is possible only as a result
of Christ's Cross; no one can arrogate it to himself. But
someone who is called to it can "take over God's grace".

The Russian poet's lover writes to him, in his hour of
hopeless abandonment in prison, the redeeming words:

> I realized with extreme clarity that death and ruin are noth-
> ing but forms of love—the final, irresistible forms of it. I
> understood—no, I beheld the unveiled mystery that in the
> immense sacrifices of our days not only our human life and
> being but also the life and being of our entire culture is par-
> ticipating and must participate—I grasped that the horren-
> dous gifts that a darkened world today is offering to destruction
> out of hatred and despair must be transformed by us, who do
> not share this hatred and despair, into sacrifices of love and
> hope. I consented to this transformation. (163f.)

"The sacrificial flame" of love alone is capable "of rais-
ing the dead to life" (166), for it is that "Paschal kiss of old
Russia" in which the poet could no longer believe.

Misericordias Domini

Christians are charged with heeding "the signs of the times". What this discernment can be like today has been shown to us with rare prophetic clarity by Gertrud von Le Fort. I would like to call it the "Paschal reading" of history (and of the present). History is not, in the final analysis, the necessarily impossible tragedy of life, because ever since Golgotha the hidden trail guiding it has been the victory of crucified love. Gertrud von Le Fort tried in her historical novels and stories to uncover this trail in the crises and upheavals of history. A theological treatise rarely succeeds in being sensitive to the reality of the mystery in the way in which the mystery of the Petrine ministry and of the Church is viewed in *Der Papst aus dem Ghetto* [The pope from the ghetto]; in the way in which light is shed on the drama of schism in *Die Magdeburgische Hochzeit* [The wedding in Magdeburg]. While theologians get muddled in questions about the "structures of the Church", she addresses their reality directly in these narratives. When theology fails in its duty to interpret history as this fine mesh woven of grace and response, of the victorious defeats of powerless love, then literature will do it, often without knowing it. For such "remedial reading" is also the writer's business.

In the "irresistible urge" of writers "to welcome the ostracized and the condemned, even the guilty who have been condemned, to accompany those who have gone astray along their path to the abyss, to press to their hearts what is declining and dying" (WG 90f.), Gertrud von Le Fort sees an oft-hidden, unsuspected orientation of literature to Christianity. Hence she firmly trusts that even in an apparently de-Christianized world, literature will track down the hidden trail of the "heart of the world", of crucified Love, for "genuine poetry unshakably remains the great lover of the guilty and the lost" (WG 93). Of course, when literature begins to make "moral arrangements", when it is rated by its ideological prognosticating and the concomitant moral disarmament, its sense for this trail is lost (WG 92f.).

No ideology, no fashion, no power, and no crisis of the Church will ever succeed in burying this trail completely; for Gertrud von Le Fort, this is no human hope but a certainty of faith. For "the appearance of Christ means that once and for all a line has been drawn by God among men between sheer success, on the one hand, and the world of pure righteousness and retribution, on the other hand, and redeeming mercy has been exalted upon the throne" (WG 91).

In her memoirs, the writer says that her first trip to church occurred on *Misericordias Domini* Sunday—she herself did not remember that, but her mother told her later. So that was the first word that the voice of the Church spoke to her: "The mercies of the Lord I will sing forever" (Ps 89:1). Gertrud von Le Fort remained faithful to that voice.

The Theme of the Battle
in C. S. Lewis' *Space Trilogy*

There is nothing more boring than to be sitting at a social gathering where some people are excitedly conversing about a film that you yourself have not seen. You hear enthusiastic exclamations, such as: "And the scene at the shore, when she slowly turns toward him—wasn't that great?"—"Yes, and then the scene with the old farmer." So the conversation goes, and I am sitting there, not knowing a thing about either "him" or "her", and with no idea as to what shore and what farmer they mean, much less the plot of the film; I cannot talk with the others and yet am supposed to feign interest. So I sit there and yet am not a part of it.

So it might be for many people when others talk about the hunt for the Hnakra, the fierce duel between Ransom and Weston, or the horrible, bloody banquet that caused the downfall of Belbury. For the "insider", a reference to this or that scene suffices to bring the whole thing vividly to mind again: for instance, the landing on Malacandra or the floating islands on Perelandra or the unique atmosphere in Saint Anne's, with "Mr. Bultitude" the bear, the good-natured, kindly Mother Dimble, the eccentric Scotsman MacPhee, and the other inhabitants of that island of peace.

November 21, 1984, lecture given at a C. S. Lewis conference, Basel.

In order to spare the "outsider" this boredom, I will recount briefly the plot of the three novels. Such a telegraphic summary can by no means replace the experience of reading them. Then I will examine more closely several motifs of the battle, so that we can then ask ourselves what we are supposed to make of this whole story.

The three novels in telegraphic style

Everything begins quite harmlessly in the first volume, *Out of the Silent Planet*. Elwin Ransom, a philologist from Cambridge, is walking through a rainy, rural district, looking for overnight accommodations. He stumbles upon a strange dwelling.

> The residents, the great physicist Weston and his assistant, a man named Devine, who proves to be a schoolmate of Ransom, are about to start a second trip to Mars in their spaceship. It so happens that they need a third man, because the inhabitants of Mars have demanded, as they think (erroneously, as it later turns out), that they bring a victim with them. The two quickly agree to the criminal plan. When Ransom awakens from unconsciousness, he finds himself in a capsule speeding through interplanetary space, in the company of his two abductors, the fanatic Weston, who wants to achieve for the human race the supreme triumph of progress, propagation through the universe, and the businessman Devine, who sees in space colonization a profitable enterprise. After the landing on Mars, Ransom manages to escape and, left to himself, enters into a friendly, hospitable relationship with the Hrossa. He learns their language and is enlightened by them concerning the nature of the planet, called Malacandra, and of its inhabitants. They all resemble animals but are endowed with speech. They form a peaceful community under their ruler, Oyarsa,

who is descended from the race of spiritual beings called
the eldila.[1]

Oyarsa in turn is subject to Maleldil. On Malacandra the
gigantic Sorns live in the icy heights of the Martian sur-
face; the Hrossa, poets and farmers, live in the valley, in the
deep furrows of the planet, and still deeper below dwell the
crafty, dwarfish Pfifltriggi.

C. S. Lewis' (d. 1963) story-telling exuberance, for all its
imaginativeness, is not purely arbitrary. There is something
so realistic about Ransom's adventures in this completely
different world that the fiction never loses the atmosphere
of actuality. "Anyone who can describe Malacandra or Perelandra in that way must have been there himself", a friend
of Ransom's says on one occasion.

Ransom learns that Thulcandra, our planet Earth, has an
Oyarsa, too, who rules it, but cruelly and destructively,
because he himself is corrupt. Ransom learns that the Oyarsa
of Thulcandra, the "Bent One", is trying to bring that corruption to other planets also through men. And so gradually he begins to understand that it was not at all by chance
that he arrived in Malacandra. The attack fails, and the three
space travelers come back to earth in a dramatic return voyage. For Ransom that was an apprenticeship. C. S. Lewis
says, "The first book is Ransom's *enfance* [childhood]." [2]

The battle now begins in earnest. "A second attack is
directed against the planet Venus, called Perelandra." [3] *Perelandra* is also the title of the second volume in the trilogy.[4]
Whereas Malacandra was an old, ancient world that is

[1] H. Kuhn, "C. S. Lewis: Der Romancier der unerbittlichen Liebe", in
Schriften zur Ästhetik (Munich, 1966), 416f.

[2] Roger Lancelyn Green and Walter Hooper, *C. S. Lewis: A Biography*, rev.
ed. (London, 1974), 179.

[3] G. Kranz, *C. S. Lewis: Studien zu Leben und Werk* (Bonn, 1974), 75.

[4] C. S. Lewis, *Perelandra* (1944; Scribner Classics Edition, 1996).

drawing near its end, Perelandra is a very young world. This time Ransom does not fly in a spaceship; he is dispatched by the eldila (a fascinating alternative to UFO's). Perelandra is "perfect beauty, ... ineffable, ripe sweetness", islands that float as though dancing, plants, trees, fruits—everything is a pleasure never before experienced, without remorse and without greed. There Ransom meets "the Green Lady". She and the "King" are the sole human inhabitants of Perelandra. "Beautiful, naked, shameless, young—she was obviously a goddess: but then the face, the face so calm that it escaped insipidity by the very concentration of its mildness, the face that was like the sudden coldness and stillness of a church when we enter it from a hot street—that made her a Madonna." The human couple on Perelandra is unacquainted with evil. The Fall has not taken place in that world. Ransom gradually understands that he was sent to this young world to preserve them from the Fall, and since he encounters only the "Lady", the battle will be over her. Weston appears as the adversary, this time no longer as a fanatical, utopian professor, but as the pliant instrument of the "Bent One"; it becomes increasingly clearer that he is now a hollow shell of a man, devoid of personality. In their pleas and counterpleas, the two earthlings try to corrupt the "Lady" or to warn her. When words prove to be less and less effective, Ransom understands that he must fight a duel to the death with Weston. In breathtaking suspense we follow the bloody duel, first on the floating islands, then in the sea, and at last, in a final crescendo, in the deep caverns of the underworld. Ransom wins and kills Weston. He hurls him into the fiery pit in the depths. In a grand concluding vision, the young world shines in the splendor of the royal human couple who have been preserved from the Fall, in the middle of an unbroken, magnificent world. Yet Ransom's victorious battle leaves a lasting, bloody mark behind: an untreatable wound on his heel.

The third volume, *That Hideous Strength*, takes place on earth. Everything begins routinely: with a faculty meeting in which the progressive forces once again take the conservatives by surprise. And with a marriage "which had become dysfunctional, or rather, had never been functional".[5] This is actually a love story that has a happy ending. And the story of two quite average young Britishers—Mark, a young university instructor of sociology, who is a bit too fond of running with the pack so as to be with the "in" crowd, and Jane, who studied at the university but did not complete a degree and now, as a disappointed young wife, does not know what she really wants, only that she definitely wants no children, so that she can still lead her own life— the story of this couple becomes the focus of a decisive battle that assumes cosmic proportions. Next there is a thoroughly modern institute known by its acronym, N.I.C.E., the "National Institute of Coordinated Experiments". Belbury is its headquarters; its goal is to establish a technocratic dictatorship; the means to this end are influential financial players, a comprehensive infiltration of the media, and an efficient and trigger-happy private police force, led by the stout, cigar-smoking Miss Hardcastle. Mark Studdock falls under the spell of the Institute; from one weakness to the next, he slides farther and farther into the clutches of the Institute, until the only choice left for him is between total compliance or being liquidated.

Jane Studdock, waiting in frustration for Mark, who comes home late and often not at all, is having dreams. And to her great alarm she discovers that she dreams real things. She sees in a dream what is happening someplace right now,

[5] Kuhn, "C. S. Lewis", 425.

and what she sees is so terrible that she is frightened and seeks help. She finds it in the plump, motherly wife of Professor Dimble. Through the Dimbles she arrives at Saint Anne's. Wonderful Saint Anne's! A country house far away, up in the highest hills, enclosed by a wall, it usually basks in the sunlight, unlike foggy Belbury. And what a strange world appears there to Jane. We have already mentioned Mr. Bultitude, the tame bear. Two married couples, the Dennistons—the same age as the Studdocks—and the Dimbles, the ever-critical MacPhee—a Scotsman—the stiff Miss Ironwood, Ivy Maggs, who is actually Jane Studdock's former cleaning lady, whose husband is in jail, and finally the Director, no other than Dr. Ransom, the undisputed leader of this little band. Belbury and Saint Anne's, it turns out, are the two "headquarters". Of course, anyone who has gone along on the journeys to Malacandra and Perelandra will not be surprised to find that here, too, other forces are in play. Whereas in the first two books it was the Oyarsa of Thulcandra, "the Bent One", who started the attacks on the worlds of Malacandra and Perelandra, now people are preparing for the great counterattack. Both camps are arming for the final battle. Belbury and Saint Anne's are the terrestrial "landing fields", for both powers need human mediums by which to intervene. Mark is drawn into Belbury only because the powers standing behind the directors and scientists of N.I.C.E. want to possess Jane, Mark's wife: her prophetic dreams are important to them, and Mark is only the decoy meant to lure Jane. Saint Anne's, too, needs Jane. The main reason that both sides need Jane, however, is that they hope to get the collaboration of yet another power. According to the old legend (which for C. S. Lewis means "in fact"), Merlin, the wizard from King Arthur's circle who is shrouded in mystery, lies buried under the spring in Bragdon Wood, not dead but asleep. His ancient Druid powers are supposed to help Belbury achieve that combination of magic and technology that will make total dictatorship possible. Merlin, awakened from his centuries-long sleep, goes over to the good side and comes to Saint Anne's. Ransom turns out to be King Arthur's successor, and the Pendragon of Logres proves to be the Fisher-King (whom we know from Wolfram von Eschenbach's *Parzival* as King Anfortas), the heir of King Arthur's realm, which never completely vanished. Merlin infiltrates Belbury, where, in a gruesome, grandiose finale, a festive banquet turns into a devastating bloodbath. The "Hideous Strength" is conquered, the Director is carried off, Mark has not only survived but has come to his senses and is a new man. The whole story ends in bed, in the self-giving that Jane and Mark have learned, during their respective journeys, in their real wedding night.

The reader wonders, though, at the conclusion: Was all that necessary just to restore order to the marriage of a young, ambitious intellectual with a somewhat frustrated young Puritan lady? Do heaven and hell have to move so mightily in order to lead to a happy ending in the marriage bed? Has C. S. Lewis brought us through the vast expanses of the universe and caused heavenly spirits to come down to earth and awakened legendary figures of the prehistoric past from their sleep so as to allow two insignificant children of Adam to discover love? It gives a strong impression of disproportion. The extravagance seems in no way related to the result. Yet it is perhaps this disturbing impression that can now help us get on the right track and tackle our topic, the theme of the battle.

The battle: An investigation of particular motifs

I do not intend to take inventory of the various motifs in the novel or to analyze them individually and pedantically; instead, I will focus specifically on the journey that Mark

and Jane make. There were battles, of course, on Malacandra and Perelandra, too. Yet those battles were a sort of
"prologue in heaven". They are Ransom's apprenticeship,
and in the first place it is not very likely that anyone present
here will be sent on similar voyages and meet with adventures like those of Dr. Ransom on Mars and Venus. In contrast, the battles of two such average people as Mark and
Jane are much closer to our own experience.

Their journey could almost be ours. Or maybe it is? How
did Mark end up in the hell of Belbury, and how did he
get back out? What caused Jane to break out of the prison
of her self-pity and fear of self-giving? Let us begin with
Jane's journey.

The novel begins with a scene in Jane and Mark's apart-
ment. Jane is alone. Mark is at the university, in his college. Is that what marriage is supposed to be? "In reality
marriage had proved to be the door out of a world of
work and comradeship and laughter and innumerable things
to do, into something like solitary confinement".[6] Is there
some way out? Jane's dissertation? She does not have the
momentum for it. Her thoughts turn around in a circle:
bitter about Mark, she is especially sorry for herself. She
takes up the morning newspaper and sees to her horror
the face of a man who is sentenced to death. She has seen
that very face quite clearly the previous night in a dream.
Is she sick, hysterical, or does she need psychoanalysis? In
her distress she seeks help and—by a strange coincidence—
comes by the address of Miss Ironwood, in "Saint Anne's
on the Hill". Despite an inner reluctance, she travels there.
What Jane hears in the strange country house in Saint
Anne's from the stiff Miss Ironwood is so strange that, as a

[6] C. S. Lewis, *That Hideous Strength* (1945; Scribner Classics Edition, 1996),
11–12.

reasonable woman, she is alarmed. No, she is neither hysterical nor sick; rather, she has the gift of prophecy, the ability to see real events in a dream. There is no cure for that, because prophecy is not an illness (64). Moreover Jane is a more important person than she herself imagines (63). Miss Ironwood invites Jane candidly and clearly to place her gift at "our" disposal (66). Jane's reaction is an interior battle, which will continue now for quite some time. "I want to lead an ordinary life. I want to do my own work. It's unbearable! Why should I be selected for this horrible thing?" (65). Why me? For a long time this question will not leave her in peace. Actually it is not true at all that Jane wanted to lead an "ordinary life". Quite the opposite: she wanted to be an important person. But not like this, with paranormal vision: "But I do not *want* it", she protests (64). She is embittered by the unexpected complications that invade her life. She does not want to "be drawn in", to get "mixed up" in "all this nonsense" (70). Indeed, she simply wants to "keep up my own life" (71). "All she wanted was to be left alone" (82). Something inside her bristled against "entanglements and interferences" (70), and that was also the deeper reason why she was determined not to have a child—or not for a long time yet (71).

Yet all her efforts are of no help at all. The dreams continue, and inexorably it becomes clear that they are dreams about real things. "The bright, narrow little life which she had proposed to live was being irremediably broken into. Windows into huge, dark landscapes were opening on every side and she was powerless to shut them" (81). What she saw in her dreams was reality. And this reality intrudes upon her life, no longer only from within, but also from outside. The little university town falls more and more into the clutches of the N.I.C.E. Expropriations, murders, and the omnipresent Institute Police transform the quiet town into a noisy, cursing chaos.

Two events conquer Jane's resistance. First, her encounter with the "Director" in Saint Anne's. The significance of this meeting can be summed up in one word, a key word for C. S. Lewis: *joy*, a hitherto unknown joy, which overwhelms all the protests of self-pity and superficial egotism. One can also call it "a feeling of rightness". The reason for this joy is difficult for her to understand, of course, since it contradicts everything she learned in her modern, one-sided, superficial education. It is willingness to obey, acceptance of her uncomfortable gift of dreaming, saying Yes to the role that has unexpectedly fallen to her lot (for her prophetic dreams are to provide extremely important information in the battle against the enemies in Belbury), especially, however, a willingness to obey the Director himself. Although doubts and objections will repeatedly gnaw away at her Yes, to the very end (142f., 312, 314ff.), a second encounter will help her to be certain, in her heart of hearts, that she has joined the right camp: her arrest by the Institute Police, by Miss Hardcastle. Jane is supposed to reveal where she has just been (she was on the way home from Saint Anne's). She realizes that these are precisely the enemies of mankind against whom the Director is fighting and that at all costs she must not betray anything (152). The sadistic torture by the female police chief fails to have its intended effect. From now on Jane is completely on the Director's side, although this does not mean that her journey is at an end. Now it is just beginning in earnest. Gradually she begins to realize that her love for Mark has been full of reservations, secret reproaches, and unacknowledged contempt, that she has expected devotion and at the same time feared submission.

Jane's journey, compared with that of her husband, seems clearer and simpler, and it is, too, since it leads straight to submission to the good, and the good is always clear and simple—which causes many people to think that this path is much too simple, that it is therefore a matter for pious women and simple-minded oafs. That is a major error, as Mark will experience personally and painfully.

But before we turn to his troublesome, ghastly journey, I would like to take up another question that is discussed one momentous evening by the group at Saint Anne's: How did Jane, and how did the other members of that group, actually arrive at their decision to support the Director's cause? After some reflection, Mr. Dimble answers this question, "Well, . . . as regards myself I fully realise that the thing has come about more or less unconsciously . . . even accidentally" (195). And in turn they all declare that they came to Saint Anne's without having planned it. The Director himself puts it this way: "You and I have not started or devised this: it has descended on us—sucked us into itself, if you like. It is, no doubt, an organisation: but we are not the organisers" (196).

We often imagine that making a decision for the good somehow has to be an especially solemn moment, in top hat and tails, so to speak, with a definite before and after. And that certainly does occur, too. But that is not Jane's journey, and hers is probably the usual way. The decision takes place most often in many small steps, which only in retrospect add up to a whole, a line.

Mark's journey into the abyss of Belbury's wickedness also begins with small steps. Actually he never simply makes a decision for evil; again and again he is just too weak to resist an alluring incentive that smells of success or promised advancement. Mark has an irresistible need to be "in", to belong to the narrower inner circle where decisions are made. More precisely, Mark has, in the first place, a fear of not belonging. Any sign of being an "outsider" is "the symbol of all his worst fears" (107). Only at the very end, after the dark night of his mortal terrors as a prisoner of the Institute, does he discover that there is another, quite different sort of "insiders", and that will be a saving liberation for him.

First of all, Mark wants to belong to the "Progressive Element" at his college. It flatters him that he is included in the "we" of this circle (15), he thinks that it is "smart" to join in the edgy, blunt language of that circle. He plays along: anything rather than be one of those people who have nothing to say, like that Hingest, who may be an important scientist but does not belong to the "in" crowd. On one occasion Mark writes just in passing, "I wish [Hingest] could be moved to a better world." It was meant in jest, as was quite common in the progressive circle (206). And so Mark accepts an invitation to join Belbury, and although an almost inaudible interior voice repeatedly tells him that the prevailing atmosphere there is dreadful, he gets involved, step by step, in a world full of mistrust, contempt, and hatred. The memory of Jane and her so completely different manner continues to prick his conscience, and when the authorities in Belbury demand that he send for his wife, he realizes that Jane and the world of Belbury do not go together and that he could not "play along" if he had Jane right there with him. Yet at first Mark is blinded by being part of it all, the feeling of power. He becomes a journalist for the Institute, writes for the major newspapers, writes things that he knows are not correct—worse, he stage-manages events by manipulating the press.

> This was the first thing Mark had been asked to do which he himself, before he did it, clearly knew to be criminal. But the moment of his consent almost escaped his notice; certainly, there was no struggle, no sense of turning a corner.... [F]or

him, it all slipped past in a chatter of laughter, of that intimate laughter between fellow professionals, which of all earthly powers is strongest to make men do very bad things before they are yet, individually, very bad men. (127)

Although Mark did not perceive it as turning a corner, in reality he did in fact cross a line. Of course, one man from the inner circle of Belbury ("Just between ourselves ... There are wheels within wheels" [109]) had clearly told him long ago, "If you try to be neutral you become simply a pawn." That is why "it is of such immense importance to each of us to choose the right side", and the choice is clear: we want to be "on the winning side" (40). "There are only two alternatives," the female police chief explains to him, "either to be in the N.I.C.E. or to be out of it" (95). But for someone who was once "in", being "out of it" means that his life is "nasty, poor, brutish, and short" (110). Especially short! That was the experience of Professor Hingest, the one whom Mark "in jest" wanted to dispatch to the next world and whom the Institute Police then in fact kill when he no longer wants to be "in". Mark's letter with the "joke" about Hingest is produced so as to indict him for the murder of his colleague. The joke has become deadly earnest. Now there is no way out. Mark has been caught in the spider web. Gradually it dawns on him that he faces two increasingly inescapable alternatives: if he goes away, the all-powerful Institute will send him to the gallows; if he remains in it to save his skin, even that will belong to them and he will be entirely at their mercy. So for the time being his journey can only lead farther inside, into the innermost circle of hellish Belbury—perhaps of hell itself. Mark is initiated. He is brought into the presence of the "Head", the diabolical counterpart of the Director at Saint Anne's: a head, a face with a brain, and nothing more, artificially kept alive with the most sophisticated technology. And this Head speaks. It demands that Jane come to Belbury. Mark makes an attempt to break out of this hell but fails. The initiation continues inexorably. Mark learns that the Institute is in the service of higher powers, the Macrobes. It dawns on him that the rulers of N.I.C.E. are themselves slaves, ruled by the evil power. So this is the innermost circle to which he wanted by all means to belong! A second attempt to flee ends in his capture. Yet his fear of being expelled still draws him back under the spell of that infernal world.

One error, though, slips by the directors of the Institute. They have not reckoned with the effect of mortal terror. In his cell, alone, he faces death, and his eyes are opened. He sees all at once what the Institute really is. "What had now taken the blinkers off was the fact that nothing *could* be done. They were going to hang him. His story was at an end. There was no harm in ripping up the web now for he was not going to use it any more" (243). During the long hours of his mortal terror, the truth gradually trickles into his mind. He sees himself, sees what sort of circle he wanted to be "in" even yesterday. How he could have trusted these people in the first place (245). Mark knows now that at all costs he must not let go of this insight (252). A new feeling: the approval of one's own conscience (265). It brings happiness and inebriates. And then Mark discovers something he set aside earlier with intellectual scorn, contrary to his feelings: simple normalcy (297). In contrast to the world of Belbury, in which everyone, from highest to lowest, lives in constant fear and clings to the others in a symbiosis of hatred, the "idea of the Straight or the Normal ... grew strong and more solid in his mind till it had become a kind of mountain" (307); this was "his first deeply moral experience" (297). The Normal: the simple people he remembers seeing in the tavern in the village of Cure Hardy

(86), the beauty of the landscape, to which Jane began to make him sensitive at the beginning of their love. The Normal works now as an antidote, strengthening his inner powers of resistance against the whole tissue of lies of the powers of N.I.C.E. When Belbury sinks into the chaos of self-destruction through Merlin's curse, Mark has already sloughed off the evil power. He is a new man, and yet still the old Mark, the genuine and normal one who now finds his way to Saint Anne's, to Jane, to his wife, to newborn love.

Now I have done something that I originally did not intend to do at all: I have started narrating, and instead of offering an analysis of individual motifs, I have traced once more the path that separated Jane and Mark and then led them back together again. And I face anew the question of whether the tremendous extravagance of all these spirits and powers was really necessary for this love story. Or should we perhaps turn the question around? Are such powers in play in the first place? Here, if not sooner, we must ask ourselves the question: What do these powers that stand behind Belbury and Saint Anne's signify? Are they real powers? Or are they simply mythical, poetic elements in C. S. Lewis' writing, that form of literary exaggeration that is necessary in order to get the reader's attention?

The evil power and the power of good

In works by C. S. Lewis, there is good and evil; heaven and hell exist, and there are angels and devils. The bewildering thing about it, though, is the fact that in his novels there are in addition human "exponents" of the two sides. Are there really supposed to be "good people" and "bad people", such Westons, Frosts, and Withers, who have simply sold themselves to the "Macrobes", which are totally subservient to the "evil power"? Where does that lead? To an end of all tolerance? And then the argument: It must be possible to speak reasonably with the people from Belbury, with a bit of kindness and patience!

What presumption it is, furthermore, simply to believe that one is on the "right" side and can clearly distinguish the right from the wrong side. Do the people in Saint Anne's think they have a monopoly on the truth? Where does that leave love of enemy? And should we start seeing the devil at work everywhere? We can, of course, evade these questions once again and say that C. S. Lewis is telling stories here and that reality is quite different. But C. S. Lewis contradicts that quite emphatically. In a radio program during the war he once said,

> I know someone will ask me, "Do you really mean, at this time of day, to re-introduce our old friend the devil—hoofs and horns and all?" Well, ... I am not particular about the hoofs and horns. But in other respects my answer is "Yes, I do." I do not claim to know anything about his personal appearance. If anybody really wants to know him better I would say to that person, "Don't worry. If you really want to, you will. Whether you'll like it when you do is another question." [7]

That is precisely what he intends: to reintroduce the devil, or more precisely, to call him by name again. The evil power of Belbury is science fiction, but, as the French say, "La réalité dépasse la fiction" (truth is stranger than fiction). Alcasan's head is no longer a utopia, and the Professor Filostratos are already capable of putting the heart of an ape into a human being. Soon they will be transplanting heads. There are plenty of Belburys, but there are also places like Saint Anne's. And the battle between the two plays itself

[7] C. S. Lewis, *Mere Christianity*, conclusion of bk. 2, chap. 2.

out in a way that is not essentially different: it begins, to all appearances, quite harmlessly, like Ransom's hike on a rainy night. Without our having deliberately sought it, we become entangled, drawn in. Whether we are liberal or conservative, highly educated or "quite normal", we cannot get around making a choice: Belbury or Saint Anne's. In a neutral country like Austria, it is difficult to believe that we cannot remain neutral. In a society that constantly talks about peace, it is difficult to grasp that there is no way to get around the battle. For the world in which we live is "territory occupied by the enemy", as C. S. Lewis says. Whether we want to or not, we must fight. We are free, but only to choose the camp, not the battle.

Reading C. S. Lewis starts quite harmlessly, too. You pick up a novel and begin to read. Since it is suspenseful and also entertaining, you allow yourself to get engrossed in the story. And suddenly you notice that you are mixed up in an adventure for which you were not looking at all. You feel like Bilbo, Tolkien's hobbit, into whose cozy dwelling adventure relentlessly intrudes one day. The reader turns into another player. He becomes entangled in "nonsense", like a passerby who gets caught up in a demonstration, or like that man from Cyrene, who on his way home from his field was suddenly detained so as to help a Galilean carry his cross.... Let it be said as a warning: It will do no good, then, to complain. "I was comfortable, in slippers, reading in the easy chair; how did I manage to get mixed up in this story? Mr. Lewis, you must have the wrong address! I just wanted to read a suspenseful novel." Too late: You are already in the middle of the story, in a very suspenseful story, in which you in particular are needed, not as a spectator, but rather as a fellow soldier, or, as C. S. Lewis says, as a "partisan". What the subsequent stages of this adventure will be like, well: "This is another story." (See the conclusion of *Out of the Silent Planet*.)

"I am going to my beloved"

C. S. Lewis' Last Novel, *Till We Have Faces*

Do gods exist? An odd question! Someone who does not believe in God will certainly not believe in gods. Someone who believes in the one God will not tolerate any gods beside him. But if there are no gods, then the ancient pagans who believed in many gods were simply in error. They honored and worshipped mythical beings when in reality there were no such things at all. They built temples for gods that did not exist.

Can we be satisfied with this answer? If the pagan belief in gods was simply false, then for thousands of years men simply prayed into the void, offered sacrifices, and celebrated feasts that were intended for no one. Well, then, are there gods after all? If we must answer Yes, does not the whole biblical faith in God start to sway?

Although C. S. Lewis was a believing, professing Christian, he also believed in the existence of the old pagan gods. Anyone familiar with his novels knows that in reading them you have to be prepared for many surprises. In his children's books we find the mysterious land of Narnia, where the animals and even the trees speak; there are planets that are inhabited—and by such strange creatures! It is not surprising that in the worlds of C. S. Lewis there are nymphs

Previously unpublished manuscript.

and elves, heroes from legendary times (Merlin) and celestial beings (the angelic *eldila*). In his last novel, which he wrote in 1958, five years before his death, things may get too confused even for inveterate C. S. Lewis fans. For in this book the ancient gods appear bodily in an extremely personal way—not only that, they even do things that happen in the old myths of the peoples, although Plato and other wise men of antiquity already found them embarrassing. For instance, the unspeakably beautiful (and terrible) young god Amor actually appears, takes an especially beautiful child of man, Psyche, as his bride, lives with her, and comes to her in the night to embrace her lovingly. And C. S. Lewis relates this as a true, real story, in which all the characters believe at the end of the novel, even those who doubted at first. C. S. Lewis was obviously intent on convincing us, too, his readers, of the truth of his story.

Therefore it is not surprising that the novel *Till We Have Faces* leaves many readers with a big question mark. No doubt it is a marvelously beautiful novel and masterfully told, perhaps the most finished of C. S. Lewis' works. But what are these stories about the gods supposed to mean? What are we to make of this world full of myths, which for C. S. Lewis seems nevertheless to be an entirely real world? Do gods exist? After reading *Till We Have Faces*, we can no longer turn our backs on this question. What answer does C. S. Lewis himself give?

The novel is based on the old myth about Amor and Psyche, about the love and sorrows of the beautiful princess Psyche and her celestial lover and spouse Amor, or Cupid, the son of Venus, the goddess of beauty. Since antiquity this myth about the love between a child of man and the son of a deity has inspired poets and painters. The theme is attractive. Is there not a divine mystery in every love? Is Psyche not the image of the human soul (*psyche* is Greek for "soul") that longs for God's love? One can interpret the myth of Amor and Psyche as an allegory, as a symbol of love, of the love between people, but especially of the love between God and man.

C. S. Lewis goes a step farther. He narrates this myth as a true, real-life story that actually happened once, at a particular place and at a particular time. For many a reader, this approach is shocking.

The life of Orual of Glome

A sketch of the storyline follows. The book is a sort of confession, an account of the life of Queen Orual of Glome, a kingdom in the Northeast in pre-Christian times. The men of her time considered her "the most wise, just, valiant, fortunate and merciful of all the princes known in our parts of the world".[1] How differently the great Queen Orual sees her own life! Bitter but also majestic in tone, her account of her life is one great indictment: Orual relentlessly levels one accusation after another against the gods. And this is the matter of her indictment: The gods have stolen away her dearest one, the only thing she had in her life: Psyche, Orual's youngest sister, the delight of her youth. They were three sisters, Orual, Redival, and Psyche, daughters of the barbaric King of Glome, who had no son. A Greek, who was sold as a slave in that distant, barbaric land, is her schoolmaster. He raises the king's daughters in the enlightened spirit of Greek wisdom: The gods, he teaches, are free from envy. The old religion of Glome sees things otherwise: Ungit, the goddess of Glome, is jealous and sinister, yet consolingly close to mankind.

[1] C. S. Lewis, *Till We Have Faces: A Myth Retold* (San Diego, New York, and London: Harcourt Brace & Co., 1956, 1984), 308f. The page references are to this edition.

There is something mysteriously beautiful about Psyche, even as a child. Her radiance attracts people. When famine and pestilence befall Glome, the people come to Psyche as if to a goddess to obtain blessings. Is it human jealousy that begrudges Psyche this attention, or is it the envy of the gods? Ungit and her priests demand that Psyche be sacrificed, or else famine and pestilence will not recede from Glome. Psyche must be sacrificed to the god of the Mountain, who is beast and beauty in one, a monster and the god of love at the same time. Psyche consents to the sacrifice, fearful and yet happy to free her land from the plague and to be wedded to the god of the Mountain, as they promise her.

The thought of losing Psyche, the sister whom she loves fervently, drives Orual to despair. She hates the gods who steal her beloved away—if they exist at all, if they are not, as the Greek says, merely images of the soul. So Psyche is abandoned on the mountain and thus handed over to the god. And behold: the pestilence comes to a halt, rain pours down, the famine is ended. Now something unbelievable happens: a few days after the sacrifice, Orual secretly goes into the mountains, where she finds Psyche alive, radiant, and happy. Psyche describes to her sister how the god came, set her free, and took her with him. Now she is married to him—his wife. Can we blame Orual for being reluctant to believe it, indeed, unable to believe it? Has Psyche perhaps gone mad? Her obvious happiness and her health suggest otherwise. Is he whom she takes for a god, who comes to her at night, perhaps a common scoundrel from the mountains, a loathsome monster? Is that why he has forbidden Psyche to see his face? Is that why he comes to her only in the dark of night? Orual assails Psyche with her doubts, unwilling to believe that everything her younger sister says about her happiness and the love of the god is real and true. Orual is unrelenting; she urges her sister to shine a lamp at night on the face of her sleeping lover, so as to see whether he is the god she supposes him to be or rather a common vagrant. Orual threatens suicide if her sister does not yield to her demand. Psyche gives in to this emotional blackmail, knowing full well that she is thereby destroying her own happiness. The following night Psyche shines a lamp on the countenance of the sleeping god. A terrific storm rips through the silence of the night, Orual hears Psyche hurrying away in tears, and then the god himself appears to her in unspeakable, unbearable glory and pronounces his judgment: "Now Psyche goes out in exile. Now she must hunger and thirst and tread hard roads.... You, woman, shall know yourself and your work. You also shall be Psyche" (173–74).

Orual knows now that the gods exist; she also knows that Psyche really was the bride of the god. But now it is too late. Psyche must wander from one land to another, weeping for her beloved. And Orual must spend the long years of her life joylessly, disconsolately, in the knowledge of her guilt. Externally her life is that of the great, righteous, wise Queen of Glome. In her inmost heart, however, the indictment lives on: Why did the gods steal Psyche away from her? Why are the gods so unjust? First they give men what they love best, and then they take it away. Why do the gods not show themselves more clearly? Is it not cruel that they allow a person to grope in the dark, but if he makes one wrong decision, they punish him as though he ought to have seen everything clearly?

Queen Orual concludes her life story with an outrageous challenge to the gods: "Let them answer my charge if they can. It may well be that, instead of answering, they'll strike me mad or leprous or turn me into beast, bird, or tree. But will not all the world then know ... that this is because they have no answer?" (249–50).

The abyss of selfish love

So much for the story. It is strange enough! What is it try-ing to say? What is its meaning?

Professor Gisbert Kranz, who has done much to make C. S. Lewis known in German-speaking countries, refers to a let-ter in which C. S. Lewis provides the key to his novel. It is a question of the old and ever-new problem of "vocation". God's demand breaks into the life of a man. A young man, for exam-ple, wants to become a missionary, a priest, or simply a Chris-tian. His relatives and friends "suffer a sense of outrage. What they love is being taken from them! The boy must be mad! And the conceit of him! Or is there something in it after all? Let's hope it is only a phase! ... Oh come back, come back, be sensible, be the dear son we used to know" (*Letters*, 274). By this example C. S. Lewis explains what matters most to him in the character of Orual: "A 'case' of human affection in its natural condition, true, tender, suffering, but in the long run, tyrannically possessive and ready to turn to hatred when the beloved ceases to be its possession. What such love particu-larly cannot stand is to see the beloved passing into a sphere where it cannot follow" (ibid.).

Psyche slips away from Orual's love. From her childhood Psyche has borne within her a longing to which Orual has no access: it draws her to the mountain where, according to the people's belief, the god lives. When Psyche is sup-posed to be sacrificed to the god on the mountain, so as to free Glome from its distress, Psyche gladly consents, despite her childish fear. To her desperate sister she says on the eve of the sacrifice: "For indeed it now feels not like going, but like going back. All my life the god of the Mountain has been wooing me. Oh, look up once at least before the end and wish me joy. *I am going to my lover.* Do you not see now—?" (76).

"It was as if someone or something else had come in between us" (75), Orual remembers, and she senses that it is not so much the gods who envy her for loving Psyche (28), but rather she herself was the one who begrudged the gods their love for Psyche (75). Psyche was supposed to belong to her, to her alone (169f., 292). In the depths of her heart she accuses the gods of only one thing: that they stole Psyche's love from her (290). Orual cannot bear it that Psyche's love for the god of the Mountain, that the god's love for Psyche, should be true and real, as true as love can ever be, truer than all the meager love that people give one another. That is Orual's indictment against the gods: "We want to be our own. I was my own and Psyche was mine and no one else had any right to her" (291f.).

The story that C. S. Lewis tells is the story of a love that has not learned to set the beloved free, one that confuses loving with having or owning. Orual's love for Psyche is above all self-love. Orual herself complains about her own loss, her pain (124). Because Psyche will not and cannot belong to her, Orual's love turns into hatred. She would rather see Psyche unhappy while possessing her than lose her in a way that would make the girl happy; she would rather see Psyche dead than alive with the gods and no longer belonging to her. And thus her love-hate finally reaches the point where she casts Psyche down into unhappiness so as not to have to admit that someone else has made Psyche happy.

C. S. Lewis has masterfully explored the abyss of this selfish love. "A love like that can grow to be nine-tenths hatred and still call itself love" (266, cf. 148). Once that happens, the rest of the love turns into grievance and accusations against one and all, against God and the world. There is no way to answer this grievance, for this complaining hears only itself, it revolves endlessly around its own self-pity; it no longer sees and accuses anyone but itself. It hears no answer but the sound of its own complaint.

Of course the novel does not end here. A postscript brings about the decisive transformation. Orual's indictment is not the last word. While she is writing down her grievance against the gods, new insights force themselves upon her awareness. In the mirror of her life story, Orual suddenly sees herself, her will to possess, her desire to have. She realizes that she has never set Psyche free, that to this day she has understood hardly anything about true love. She learns late in life how much she still has to learn about the meaning of love.

The final pages in her account of her life are visions, waking dreams, in which she must suffer through bitter, difficult trials until she is allowed to see Psyche again. Slowly it dawns on her: the answer that she could not hear in her self-centered despair. Had the god not told her, "You also shall be Psyche"? What was that supposed to mean? In her visions she begins to understand that through all the long, disconsolate years since the day when she cast Psyche down into unhappiness, she had helped by her own sorrow to bear her sister's sorrow. Nothing was wasted; nothing was suffered in vain. Now she understands that she has borne the sorrow that she caused her sister. Her jealousy dissolves; deep wounds that she has hidden for many years in her inmost heart begin to heal. Orual is ugly, very ugly. Her sister Psyche is unimaginably beautiful. Orual understands that her soul must first become beautiful, as though purified in the fire, before the pain caused by her lack of physical beauty can be healed.

Now comes the final vision: Orual finds Psyche again; joy and reconciliation! Psyche was right before her misfortune when she said to Orual, "All will be well; all will be better than you can dream of" (128f.). For now Orual is to receive an answer to all her questions. Together with Psyche she is allowed to look at the god, and in that overwhelming glory a love dawns on her that she has never known, that she has thought impossible. she recognizes why Psyche loved the god, her god: she herself has become Psyche, like Psyche, and yet completely herself.

Orual's last words, after this vision, are a prayer: "I know now, Lord, why you utter no answer. *You are yourself the answer*" (308).

The way to God

In his novel *Till We Have Faces*, C. S. Lewis has movingly depicted man's way to God. Orual looked for love; her whole life was an errant, confused search for the one and only happiness of love. She thought that she had found this happiness in her love for her sister Psyche, and when it began to slip away from her, she desperately clung to it. She suspected that the gods, the god of the Mountain, would not grant her that happiness, and finally she hated him when she was convinced that he had stolen it from her. She raged and stormed against the silence of the gods, accused them of cruelty, until at the end of her journey she was allowed to see the god again, not as an accuser, not as a judge, but rather as the answer to her lifelong search. In him she rediscovered her beloved Psyche, not in opposition to him, but in him.

Do gods really exist? Does C. S. Lewis have an answer to this question? His novel takes place in pagan antiquity. For him the gods of the heathens are not simply "nonentities". Did the Apostle Paul not speak to the Athenians about the "unknown god" whom they worshipped without knowing him (Acts 17)? C. S. Lewis, like many early Church Fathers, believed that the myths of the pagans, their stories about gods and their worship of those gods, contained glimmerings that would show their full significance only in the light of revelation, in the light of Jesus Christ.

C. S. Lewis (like Augustine), moreover, thought that the gods of the pagans were the same beings as those whom Christianity calls angels. They are all no more than signs pointing to God himself, the living, true God, who, as Paul also said in Athens, "is not far from each one of us".

What are we to make, then, of the odd story about the real, loving partnership between Psyche and "her beloved", the god of the Mountain? Is C. S. Lewis not still being a bit too "pagan" here?

Anyone who knows a little about the history of Christian mysticism knows how little Lewis, a believing Anglican, invented here. In the writings of many mystics we find the conviction that God (or Christ) enters into a real, intimate bond of love with the soul, and these mystics are not ashamed to use images of spousal love for it. Did not the Song of Songs in the Old Testament depict God's love for his people, for his bride, Israel, in the most vivid colors of a bodily love?

There is something else that C. S. Lewis is trying to show: pious pagans already knew that God's claim on the heart of man is unrelenting. As terrible as pagan human sacrifices were, they are, nevertheless—in their defective way—a testimony to the truth that man owes God, not a part, a piece of himself, but all of himself, unreservedly. Love for God demands one's whole heart, one's whole mind, one's whole soul. Psyche knew that. Therefore she was delighted to be sacrificed to the god. The martyrs in every century have known this same thing: to give everything for Christ, for God's sake, even one's bodily life, is the supreme happiness, the most sublime fulfillment.

There is one more thing to be said about C. S. Lewis' novel. At the conclusion, Psyche becomes a goddess—and yet remains herself, the radiant child of man. Orual, too, at the end of her wanderings, becomes a goddess. Once again: Is this not all too pagan? Not for someone who knows what all great teachers of Christianity have said: that God became man so that man might become God. Yes, we are all supposed to become Psyche, to become "gods", not so as to stop being men, but rather as men to become really and truly God's children, sons and daughters of God. John, the beloved disciple of Jesus, goes even farther: he says that we are already God's children (1 Jn 3:2), in other words, gods, and that of course this is still hidden, for it will be revealed only when we shall see *him*, *as* he is—he, who alone is the answer to all our questions.

Grace! Pardon! Mercy!

An Interpretation of Shakespeare's
Measure for Measure

The invitation to speak in the Burgtheater in Vienna about Shakespeare's *Measure for Measure* came as a surprise. How did it happen that I, of all people, was invited? Because the play is set in Vienna? Or was I invited because the Duke appears for almost the entire play disguised as a monk? Of course, Lucio, with his slanderous tongue, recalls the old saying, "Cucullus non facit monachum" (The cowl does not make the monk) (V, 1). I myself am a "monk" and for thirty years wore the cowl of a Dominican—or "Friar Preacher", to be precise—before I was clothed in the vestments of a bishop. Was that why they invited me? Or was it some very secret knowledge about the relations that Shakespeare had with the London cloister of the Blackfriars, as the Dominicans are called in English? Or was I invited because of the heated debate in recent scholarship over whether Shakespeare was a "crypto-Catholic" and whether this might shed a new, clearer light on many things in his plays? In their fascinating studies,[1] three

April 25, 2007, lecture in the series, "Shakespeare: A Republic of Mistakes", Burgtheater, Vienna. (First published in abridged form in the *Frankfurter Allgemeine Zeitung*, no. 115 [May 19, 2007], p. Z-1.)

[1] Debora Kuller Shuger (of Los Angeles), *Political Theologies in Shakespeare's England: The Sacred and the State in* Measure for Measure (New York: Palgrave, 2001); Clare Asquith, *Shadowplay: The Hidden Beliefs and Coded Politics of William Shakespeare* (New York: PublicAffairs, 2005); Hildegard

authors, Debora Kuller Shuger, Clare Asquith, and Hildegard Hammerschmidt-Hummel, have demonstrated Shakespeare's connections to the persecuted Catholics of the Elizabethan period, but also during the years when James I ruled England: *Measure for Measure* was first performed during his reign on the feast of Saint Stephen [December 26] in the year 1604 in Whitehall in London. Their well-researched hypotheses had no small influence on my interpretation of *Measure for Measure*. Scholars will continue to investigate the matter, and Shakespeare will be studied by many more generations—otherwise he would not be Shakespeare.

Probably the reason for the invitation was simply that *Measure for Measure* is about questions of moral rigorism, about ethical fundamentalism and its perpetual conflict with laxism, or simply about its constant breakdown in practice, and about the repeated attempts to decree morality and its lamentable failure, given the condition of human nature. What could be more reasonable than to consult on this topic someone who represents that institution to which is attributed, with a firmly anchored prejudice, that very same ethical rigorism whose failure the comedy *Measure for Measure* drastically portrays: the Catholic Church.

I am ready, therefore, to assume this role but take the liberty of "rewriting" it, of employing it for a somewhat different purpose than might be expected. I must confess that I myself am somewhat in suspense as to where this role will lead me. For the suspenseful thing about dealing with Shakespeare is, after all, that nothing fits into preconceived categories.

Hammerschmidt-Hummel, *Die verborgene Existenz des William Shakespeare: Dichter und Rebell im Katholischen Untergrund* (Freiburg: Herder, 2001). Also recommended is: Peter Milward, *Shakespeare the Papist* (Naples, Florida: Sapientia Press, 2005).

"Grace, pardon, mercy" is the title of this lecture. In order to frame the topic, I will preface my talk with a prooemium, a dramatic prologue.

Grace and disgrace on the stage

Anyone who walks onstage is at the mercy, for better or for worse, of the public's goodwill [*Gnade*]. For this reason those who put themselves on display yearn for nothing more than to find favor [*Gnade*] in the eyes of the onlookers. They hope to please, and to the extent that the spectators are gracious, they win approval and acceptance. The ones who manage to stand especially high in people's good graces are even said by the latter to be ennobled, "favored" [*begnadet*].

But God help those who fall into disgrace while onstage! The fall from the proscenium (or apron) into the pit is steep and is slowed only in the rarest falls from grace. Clemency [*Begnadigung*] for a "favored" individual who has fallen into disfavor [*Ungnade*] seldom occurs in this gracious establishment [that is, the theater].

And yet one cannot overlook the fact that the stage and grace (= favor) are interwoven. Applause is and will always be the "bread of charity" [*Gnadenbrot*] in any life dedicated to showmanship.

The opportunity to reflect on how the play *Measure for Measure* deals particularly with the themes of grace, pardon, and mercy was the main reason that I agreed and am standing here today. For I consider this "message" to be the most important one of all. "By the grace of Grace", we read in the final lines of what is probably the most merciless [*gnadenlosesten*] drama about human wickedness and entanglement in guilt, *Macbeth* (V, 8, 72). Is everything ultimately grace? Does even the most horrible tragedy end "with the grace of our gracious God", to paraphrase Shakespeare? Is there always a happy ending, or is such a view simply too naïve, too callow? Does it not trivialize the horror of the twentieth century? But does this view not trivialize Shakespeare also? Critical judgments on this question differ considerably.

Hans Urs von Balthasar, the great Swiss theologian and man of letters, sees in *Measure for Measure* the "high point of the problem of justice versus mercy [in Shakespeare]".

> This is a Christian mystery play, ... whether or not the poet intended it as such, no matter how many comic and tragic elements are mixed in with it. Shakespeare creates a highly realistic world and works toward a single final scene that occupies the whole of the fifth act: everyone is brought to judgment, and no one knows how it will end. The prospect of a happy issue is concealed from moment to moment, the scales of justice are handled gravely, and only then can the sentence be uttered, "I find an apt remission in myself" [which Baudissin translates into German with the appropriate grandeur, "Ich fühle Neigung, allen zu verzeihen" (I feel inclined to pardon everyone)].[2]

But is this really about pardoning? Is grace, *mercy*, really the theme here? Harold Bloom sees it quite differently. "I do not know any other eminent work of Western literature that is nearly as nihilistic as *Measure for Measure*, a comedy that destroys comedy",[3] "a play so savagely bitter as to be unmatched in that regard".[4] Only the perpetually drunk prisoner Barnardine finds favor in Bloom's eyes: "All that remains is the marvelous image of the dissolute murderer Barnardine, who gives

---

[2] Hans Urs von Balthasar, *Theo-drama: Theological Dramatic Theory*, vol. 1, *Prolegomena*, trans. Graham Harrison (San Francisco: Ignatius Press, 1988), 470.

[3] Harold Bloom, *Shakespeare: The Invention of the Human* (New York: Riverhead Books and Penguin Putnam, 1998), 380.

[4] Ibid. 358.

us a minimal hope for the human as against the state, for being unwilling to die for any man's persuasion." [5]

Is pardon, therefore, not really a theme here and in Shakespeare's works in general? Is King Cymbeline's remark, "Pardon's the word to all" (V, 5, 421), not a key phrase after all in understanding Shakespeare?

There is no one interpretation of Shakespeare. So I make so bold as to present my reading and to explain why I think that *Measure for Measure* is a "problem play" that does deal essentially with the power of pardoning.

Is clemency authoritarian caprice?

In my attempt to interpret Shakespeare's play, I proceed, therefore, from the thesis that "*Measure for Measure* is the Shakespearean play most closely connected with the idea of forgiveness." [6] It is the drama by Shakespeare "that not only contains the theme of forgiveness and grace but is moved and defined by it".[7] I am aware that this interpretation is quite contrary to the one just mentioned of the great Shakespeare expert Harold Bloom. But perhaps my reading will still find some favor, if not with the experts, then perhaps with you, who grant me the favor of listening to me.

In fact the theme of "grace" is found at the very beginning of the play. The Duke wishes to leave Vienna to travel. He gives Angelo full authority to represent him in all his affairs during his absence. "Mortality and mercy in Vienna live in thy tongue and heart." Angelo, therefore, has complete "power over death and clemency in Vienna" (so Frank

[5] Ibid., 380.

[6] Ernst Theodor Sehrt, *Vergebung und Gnade bei Shakespeare* (Stuttgart, 1952), 198.

[7] Ibid., 121.

Günther translates the line into German), over "capital punishment and pardon" (Walter Pache's translation).

What do clemency [*Gnade*] and pardon mean here? Before
I invite you to walk a bit with me through the play, we
should discuss first a deep-seated prejudice.

Is clemency not a barely disguised kind of arbitrary exer-
cise of authority?

Which way the scales tip, toward the death penalty or
toward pardon, seems here to lie entirely within the free
discretion of the ruler's tongue and heart. Is clemency
caprice? The Internet encyclopedia Wikipedia [in Ger-
man] is not the most reliable source, but it often gives inter-
esting insights into contemporary ways of thinking. There
we can read:

> The concept of "grace" denotes an understanding of author-
> ity in Christianity.... According to this conception, not only
> God, but every Christian authority in the believing world
> (bishops, kings, judges ... by the grace of God) is gracious
> [*gnädig*] and therefore treats those who are entrusted to its
> protection in an arbitrary and personal way depending on
> the situation and sorts them into those who are endowed
> with grace and those who have fallen into disgrace. Hence
> a binding system of law, which furthermore is intelligible
> and verifiable, ... is not at all necessary.

Hence the Wikipedia article concludes:

> Thus authoritarian forms of human society resembling dic-
> tatorships are theologically justified and reinforced. This also
> implies, on the other hand, that those under the protection
> of a given authority are in need of grace; they need the strong,
> "gracious" hand of the divine, ecclesiastical, and secular lord....
> Consequently, the subjection and control of people are willed
> by God and pleasing to God.[8]

[8] [German] Wikipedia, "Gnade", as of April 20, 2007.

No doubt all of that exists under the cloak of "grace" and "clemency": the humiliation of accepting "charity", making others dependent through the game of granting and withholding love, emotional insecurity caused by alternating waves of graciousness and rejection, the abuse of power through the non-transparent bestowal or refusal of favors [*Gnaden*]. All this is the stuff of countless dramas, because life itself plays out that way, completely unchanged, to this day.

Does Shakespeare's *Measure for Measure* belong to this world of the arbitrary "granting of favors"? Some can and do read it that way. The Duke is a ruler who belongs to the world of absolutism, in which there are no democratic checks on power, in which power is conferred by the grace of God. As sovereign, he can "enforce or qualify the laws", and so can his representative, Angelo, "as to your soul seems good" (I, 1, 65f.). With this sovereign freedom, he will administer pardon as well at the conclusion—and join together the couples who are to wed. Off with you into the safe haven of marriage! Whether that really is a happy ending is something that the play leaves unsettled.

So it is not surprising that many interpreters have difficulty with this sort of clemency. But is grace like that? Does the description in Wikipedia apply here? Everything depends on the answer to one question: Is there such a thing as genuine guilt? Only in terms of the question about guilt can we see clearly what grace and pardon can mean. Guilt is the great theme that makes the meaning of grace visible in the first place. I think there are so many prejudices against grace because the question of guilt is repressed. This usually occurs in one of two ways: either guilt is simply denied and made into "so-called evil" (Konrad Lorenz), into a part of nature, which happens to be cruel; only the fittest survive in the battle for existence; there is no good and evil, but only weak and strong; social Darwinism is the schoolmaster here. Or else guilt exists, but not in my case. Guilt cannot be denied, and so it must be delegated. Others are guilty, society, the Jews, the Americans, depending on who happens to be made the "scapegoat". Considering oneself guiltless while blaming others— our era has truly mastered this art. A third way is common also: internalizing the role of scapegoat. False feelings of guilt are the result. One is talked into having a guilty conscience, which torments and restricts freedom. The Church is often accused of doing this.

But here is a preview of the paradox that is evident in *Measure for Measure*: genuine insight into guilt becomes possible only in the realm of grace. In a merciless world, confession of guilt is impossible, indeed, lethal. You cannot live with insight into guilt without the perspective of grace. That leads to despair and suicide—as in the case of Lady Macbeth. Grace is "gratuitous", unearned, but not cheap. It is a pure gift, but it requires a ready and willing heart. This "preparation" for grace is the subject of *Measure for Measure*, as I read it. All the characters mature, step by step, through trials, failures, and judgment and become ripe for pardon and grace.

Angelo, or "Let anyone who thinks that he stands take heed lest he fall" (1 Cor 10:12)

In a morally decaying Vienna, where freedom leads justice around by the nose (I, 3, 29), Duke Vincentio, who for fourteen years (I, 3, 21) has been all too lax in ruling, decides to perform an experiment so as to find out what sort of ruler would result if he were to invest "absolute power" (I, 3, 13) in a representative. "With special soul" (I, 1, 18), as he divulges to old Lord Escalus, he appoints, after "a leavened and prepared choice" (I, 1, 52), the young Lord Angelo, "a man of stricture and firm abstinence" (I, 3, 12), for the duration of his feigned journey to Poland, so that the latter, by virtue of the "strict statutes and most biting laws" (I, 3, 19) that are still in force in Vienna, may by a mighty "ambush" enforce discipline and order while sparing the Duke's own name the "slander" that can be expected during the "fight" (I, 3, 39ff.). However, so as to be able to observe how his deputy represents him, he decides to "visit both prince and people" disguised as a monk (I, 3, 45) and to remain in the city as a sort of monastic Harun al-Rashid. "For a name" (I, 2, 173), that is, in order to make a name for himself, Angelo immediately carries out the Duke's plan "to unloose this tied-up justice" (I, 3, 32). A good opportunity presents itself: the young Lord Claudio has impregnated Juliet, who is betrothed but not married to him. According to the strict law, Angelo condemns him to death. Claudio appeals in vain to the Duke, who "is very strangely gone from hence" (I, 4, 50), and so he asks his friend Lucio, a dissolute dandy, to give his sister Isabella, who intends that day to enter a convent of Poor Clares as a novice, a report about his situation (I, 2, 184), in the hope that she might "soften" Angelo by her "fair prayer" (I, 4, 69f.).

So much for the "exposition" of the play. Who is this Angelo, whom the Duke trusts so much? In keeping with his name, he enjoys an angelic reputation. To the Duke, who seeks his counsel, old Lord Escalus says, "If any in Vienna be of worth / To undergo such ample grace and honor, / It is Lord Angelo" (I, 1, 23–25). But even angels can fall. Angelo is sure of himself. Therein lies his drama. Here he will fail, fall, and incur guilt.

Very soon Escalus sees that the deputy Angelo vastly overrates himself in his sternness toward others: Yes, it is often necessary to proceed somewhat more severely, but "rather cut a little, / Than fall, and bruise to death" (II, 1, 4f.). So he begs for mercy for young Claudio.

> Let but Your Honor know,
> Whom I believe to be most strait in virtue,
> That, in the working of your own affections,
> Had time cohered with place or place with wishing,
> Or that the resolute acting of your blood
> Could have attained the effect of your own purpose,
> Whether you had not sometime in your life
> Erred in this point which now you censure him,
> And pulled the law upon you. (II, 1, 7–16)

But Angelo acts quite sure of himself. " 'Tis one thing to be tempted, Escalus, / Another thing to fall" (II, 1, 17f.).

> When I that censure him do so offend,
> Let mine own judgment pattern out my death,
> . . . Sir, he must die. (II, 1, 28–31)

Angelo intends to put things in order. And the Vienna of this play needs that. Karl Kraus (d. 1936) had good reason for being so fond of quoting from *Measure for Measure* when he let loose with his diatribes against Viennese conditions. The "boorish" scenes supply plenty of material in this regard. All the houses of ill repute in the suburbs are to be razed. But in the red light district, the pimps and the madams in charge of the brothels (Madame Overdone) have good enough connections with the higher-ups to be able to continue to ply their trade in better quarters (I, 2, 87ff.).

Why this severity against "lechery", of all things, against *luxuria*, dissipation? Why the death penalty for Claudio's "fornication"? He slept with Juliet, with whom he was already bound by a valid but not yet public marriage contract. One of the pimps, Pompey, quite bluntly says something that would be just as true today: If this strict law is enforced, it would be necessary "to geld and splay [sterilize] all the youth of the city"

(II, 1, 241). Then, in his opinion, Vienna would be depopulated within ten years.

And the dandy Lucio expresses it in his unvarnished language: "Why, what a ruthless thing is this in him [the Governor Angelo], for the rebellion of a codpiece to take away the life of a man!" (III, 2, 121f.). Shakespeare's language in this play is nothing if not direct. Even Provost, the prison guard, sees in Angelo's stricter application of the law only senseless rigor: "Alas, he [Claudio] hath but as offended in a dream! All sects, all ages smack of this vice; and he to die for't!" (II, 2, 4–6).

Is this strict enforcement a dramatic device, or did it actually take place? Probably both! Under Puritan influence, the Old Testament ordinances concerning fornication and adultery were increasingly incorporated into the law of the State. After all, the Bible was supposed to be taken as literally as possible. Angelo is described by the Duke as "precise", a "code word" for Puritan (I, 3, 50). In the Middle Ages, which are usually and incorrectly described as dark, *luxuria*, that is, any form of extramarital sexual relations, was regarded as a sin, which was therefore to be dealt with in confession, not before the magistrate and certainly not as a capital crime. In periods when Sharia law was applied again in many places, there is evidence that such strict enforcement was quite real at the time. The Duke represents here, instead, the tolerant Catholic position, which knows that not all moral evils can be done away with by civil laws. Not only brothels but also theaters fell victim at times to radical Puritanism. One important sociopolitical message of the play *Measure for Measure* is that civil legislation that tries too inflexibly to regulate morality inevitably leads to more hypocrisy, more clandestine outlets for human weaknesses.

The Duke says at the beginning, as he puts on the monk's cowl, "Hence shall we see, / If power change purpose, what our seemers be" (I, 3, 54). Will it be possible to improve public morality through inflexible laws, through a rigorous intervention that even today is demanded again and again? And will Angelo, the strict improver of morals, use his power in such a way that it does not corrupt him?

The Duke is skeptical. He takes a look at what happens. Then he intervenes more and more, becomes the "stage manager" without whom Angelo would have caused a catastrophe. Why did he himself let things slide earlier, hold the reins too loosely?

> For we bid this be done
> When evil deeds have their permissive pass,
> And not the punishment. (I, 3, 37f.)

Freely paraphrased: when, because of permissiveness, evil acquires freedom and no longer is punished, it is taken for granted as something that must be done. Today we have certainly reached a similar point. If a lady—the Secretary of Education—distributes condoms in Austrian schools, then *luxuria* has obviously become a duty. In Shakespeare one learns to call things by their name.

The Duke, in any case, has an uneasy conscience. He has become pensive: "Sith, 'twas my fault to give the people scope" (I, 3, 35). Will "restraint" work any better? That is the question here! The Duke reminds me somewhat of our '68 generation, which now sees with apprehension that we too often allowed things to "have their permissive pass" and set aside the question of sanctions, as though the law could continue to exist even when there was no punishment. But how does one go back? How can we arrive again at greater order without falling into the excesses of Angelo's fundamentalism? Peter Sloterdijk said a while ago in an interview in *Die Zeit*, "Whereas earlier we used to think unceasingly about subversion, by now we are grateful for every iota of stable structure." [9]

Is there a humane way between permissiveness and rigorism? *Measure for Measure* could be on the right track. Angelo's overzealousness has an effect that is dramatic, in the literal sense. Suddenly the matter becomes serious. It becomes real. It ceases to be a trivial "anything goes" situation. And with that everything becomes livelier, more suspenseful. Without drama, there would be no drama! Without seriousness, there would be no theatrical play, for what is performed on the stage is as serious as real life, as inescapable as life itself. Nothing would be more banal than the fact that Claudio was in bed with his fiancée, Juliet—obviously not the subject for a play today. But here it is, because she is pregnant and he is in prison. Someone has dared to take quite literally what the strict interpretation of the Mosaic Law demands. At first there is no question as to whether Angelo has acted rightly. The one important thing is that in this situation a deed and its consequences cannot be separated. That is precisely what makes everything dramatic. Human action is not banal. It has consequences. These in fact are not always appropriate. They can, as in our present case, be disproportionate, excessive. But this happens in real life: a little cause—a big effect. A small mistake—great harm. Now the drama begins, and with it the path whose destination is called forgiveness. But let us not anticipate that. Let us turn to Claudio on his way to prison. It could have happened to any one of us. We visit ourselves in a place where we all may be tomorrow.

LUCIO: Why, how now, Claudio! Whence comes this restraint?

[9] *Die Zeit*, February 8, 2007, p. 15.

CLAUDIO: From too much liberty, my Lucio, liberty:
  As surfeit is the father of much fast,
  So every scope by the immoderate use
  Turns to restraint. Our natures do pursue,
  Like rats that ravin down their proper bane
    [= poison],
  A thirsty evil; and when we drink we die.
    (I, 2, 128–34)

Claudio is aware of his human brokenness. He can indulge in no more illusions about himself, and even though the death penalty imposed on him is utterly excessive, the inescapable seriousness of his situation serves as a "wake-up call". As Baudissin translates the speech: "Man's bent is followed … by the thirsty hour, and the drink grows deadly." "A thirsty evil"! Claudio does not begin with self-justifications; rather, he names the "law" that is at work in him as in us all and that thirsts for our failure. He is perpetrator and victim. Of all the characters of the play, he is the first to be ready for *mercy* and *pardon*. In him the conversion has already begun, even though the path will still be painful.

Angelo is different: the attempts to bring him around and to turn the death penalty into a pardon fail. They are smashed to pieces against his self-assurance. The ancient Lord Escalus makes the first attempt, which has already been mentioned. Isabella makes the second; she is the sister of the condemned man and is about to enter a cloistered convent.

Incidentally, though not irrelevant to our understanding of the play, it is rather peculiar, in a drama that was performed for King James I, that a major character wants to become a Poor Clare; since the time of Henry VIII, all the monasteries in the kingdom had been dissolved. The monks, too, who appear in the play, make a *bella figura* [a fine impression]. No trace of the Protestant criticism of monks and nuns that had been common since Luther. Moreover "Isa-bella", according to the scholars mentioned earlier, is one of Shakespeare's crypto-Catholic "code words"; in the early sixteenth century there was a nun by the name of Isabella Shakespeare who headed a convent in Wroxham, the place of origin of Shakespeare's ancestors.

Isabella, or pardon is the measure

We can summarize only the most important parts of the dramatic dialogue between Isabella and Angelo. Isabella places before Angelo's eyes a picture of power different from the one behind which he has entrenched himself.

> No ceremony that to great ones 'longs [= belongs],
> Not the king's crown, nor the deputed sword,
> The marshal's truncheon, nor the judge's robe—
> Become them with one half so good a grace
> As mercy does.
> If he had been as you, and you as he,
> You would have slipped like him; but he, like you,
> Would not have been so stern. (II, 2, 59–66)

Lord Angelo will not relent: "Your brother is a forfeit of the law, / And you but waste your words" (II, 2, 71–72). Isabella responds with an argument that in the Catholic Vienna of Duke Vincentio ought to have been the con-vincing one:

> Alas, alas!
> Why, all the souls that were were forfeit once,
> And He that might the vantage best have took
> Found out the remedy. How would you be,
> If He, which is the top of judgment, should
> But judge you as you are? O, think on that;

> And mercy then will breathe within your lips,
> Like man new-made. (II, 2, 72–78)

Angelo, however, remains adamant. Isabella therefore tries
brilliant ridicule.

> Could great men thunder
> As Jove himself does, Jove would ne'er be quiet,
> For every pelting, petty officer
> Would use his Heaven for thunder.
> Nothing but thunder! Merciful Heaven,
> Thou rather with thy sharp and sulphurous bolt
> Split'st the unwedgeable and gnarled oak
> Than the soft myrtle. But man, proud man,
> Dressed in a little brief authority,
> Most ignorant of what he's most assured,
> His glassy essence, like an angry ape,
> Plays such fantastic tricks before high Heaven
> As make the angels weep—who, with our spleens,
> Would all themselves laugh mortal. (II, 2, 111–23)

Isabella makes a deep impression on Lord Angelo. At the
end of the conversation he says to himself, aside, "She speaks,
and 'tis / Such sense, that my sense breeds with it." And
then to Isabella, "I will bethink me: come again tomorrow" (II, 2, 141–43). Yet the deep impression leads in a
direction that Lord Angelo does not expect. As she leaves,
Isabella says, "[God] save your Honor!" And he answers,
again aside:

> From thee,—even from thy virtue!
> What's this, what's this? Is this her fault or mine?
> The tempter or the tempted, who sins most?
> Ha!
> Not she; nor doth she tempt; but it is I
> That, lying by the violet in the sun,

Do as the carrion does, not as the flower,
Corrupt with virtuous season. Can it be
That modesty may more betray our sense
Than woman's lightness? Having waste ground enough,
Shall we desire to raze the sanctuary,
And pitch our evils there? O, fie, fie, fie!
What dost thou, or what art thou, Angelo?
Dost thou desire her foully for those things
That make her good? Oh, let her brother live.
Thieves for their robbery have authority
When judges steal themselves. What, do I love her,
That I desire to hear her speak again,
And feast upon her eyes? What is't I dream on?
O cunning enemy, that to catch a saint,
With saints dost bait thy hook! Most dangerous
Is that temptation that doth goad us on
To sin in loving virtue: never could the strumpet,
With all her double vigor, art and nature,
Once stir my temper; but this virtuous maid
Subdues me quite. Ever till now,
When men were fond, I smiled, and wondered how.
    (II, 2, 162–87)

The State, Angelo's own public authority, and the dignified reputation that results from his virtue become insipid
to him; he says that he will set Isabella's brother free if she
yields to him, Angelo. She is indignant. Even torture and
death threats would not bring her to do that, she says in
strongly sensual images:

ISABELLA: ... [W]ere I under the terms of death,
    The impression of keen whips I'd wear as rubies,
    And strip myself to death, as to a bed

> That longing have been sick for, ere I'd yield
> My body up to shame.
> ANGELO: Then must your brother die.
> ISABELLA: And 'twere the cheaper way:
>   Better it were a brother died at once,
>   Than that a sister, by redeeming him,
>   Should die forever. (II, 4, 100–108)

Even when Angelo threatens that her brother shall have to die a painful death if she does not yield to him, she clearly and resolutely continues to refuse: "More than our brother is our chastity" (II, 4, 185).

Hardly any sentence in this play meets today with a greater lack of understanding, indeed, with mockery and rejection. I was shocked by this lack of understanding. People do not seem to realize that Isabella's refusal to save her brother by agreeing to a de facto rape is the heart, the centerpiece, the real turning point, the "catastrophe", in which everything apparently tends toward misfortune but in reality saves the day. Just as for Claudio the death sentence becomes the saving catastrophe, so also for Isabella this courageous, misunderstood No becomes the only deed that makes true emancipation possible. It is Isabella's liberating deed. Isabella's speech after Angelo's exit is for me the great stroke of liberation, starting from which everything can turn for the better:

> O perilous mouths,
> That bear in them one and the selfsame tongue,
> Either of condemnation or approof;
> Bidding the law make courtsy to their will;
> Hooking both right and wrong to the appetite,
> To follow as it draws! (II, 4, 172ff.)

That is precisely the point: To bow to that arbitrary will is the end of freedom, the sell-out of righteousness and justice.

It makes everything caprice. Isabella's behavior is courageous and clear-sighted. She is not anxiously defending a
hymen of which she is proud. She has great understanding
for her brother's weakness: "Ask your heart", she says to Angelo,
"what it doth know / That's like my brother's fault" (II, 2,
137f.). At the conclusion she will look with forbearance upon
Angelo's "fleshly" weakness as well. But she rebels against tyranny. This makes Isabella one of those courageous women and
men who have not bowed to the wishes of the tyrant, even
when giving in would apparently have saved the day. Here,
in my estimation, is the key to the problem of rigorism vs.
laxism. They are two sides of one coin. The rigorist inter-
preter of the law Angelo suddenly proves to be a laxist and a
tyrant at the same time. The proper measure is found only
by justice that is founded on mercy.

This interpretation of Isabella, which is contrary to that
of too many literary critics, is corroborated by something
that is almost always overlooked in commentaries on *Measure for Measure*: Angelo's monstrous decision to have Isabella's brother executed despite all the assurances.

Let us return briefly to the plot of the play. Isabella hurries from her second conversation with the governor, Angelo,
to her brother in prison. In the jail, where the Duke, disguised as a monk, has prepared Claudio for death, "that
makes these odds all even", Isabella explains to her brother
that she cannot ransom him from death by sinning. Claudio agrees with her at first but then, fearing death, rebukes
her harshly. She, however, insists that she will not give in
to pressure from Angelo or allow herself to be ravished.
The Duke / Brother Lodowick has overheard the conversation and tells Claudio that Angelo never intended to abuse
his sister, and, therefore, he should prepare himself for death.
Claudio replies, "Let me ask my sister pardon" (III, 1, 173).
And "he professes to have received no sinister measure from

his judge, but most willingly humbles himself to the determination of justice" (III, 2, 255ff.).

Now comes the famous "bed trick". On the Duke's advice,
Mariana, with whom Angelo is betrothed, is presented
to him in place of Isabella. Thus "false exacting", that is,
an unlawful demand, shall be repaid "with falsehood"
(disguise)—once again, measure for measure. Angelo is to
be guilty of precisely the same thing that Claudio had done
prematurely with Juliet: sleeping with his betrothed and thus
consummating the marriage.

In Act III events unfold in rapid succession. It becomes
evident that the waistcoat of the strict Puritan Angelo was
by no means as white as he pretended—and as his public
reputation maintained.

> DUKE [*disguised as the monk Lodowick*]: [Mariana] should
> this Angelo have married, was affianced to her by
> oath, and the nuptial appointed. Between which time
> of the contract and limit of the solemnity, her brother
> Frederick was wrecked at sea, having in that per-
> ished vessel the dowry of his sister. But mark how
> heavily this befell to the poor gentlewoman. There
> she lost a noble and renowned brother, in his love
> toward her ever most kind and natural, with him
> the portion and sinew of her fortune, her marriage
> dowry, with both her combinate husband, this well-
> seeming Angelo.
>
> ISABELLA: Can this be so? Did Angelo so leave her?
> DUKE: Left her in her tears, and dried not one of them
> with his comfort; swallowed his vows whole, pre-
> tending in her discoveries of dishonor. In few,
> bestowed her on her own lamentation, which she
> yet wears for his sake, and he, a marble to her tears,
> is washed with them, but relents not. (III, 1, 221–39)

Several details in this description correspond, with keen irony, to the crime that Lord Angelo intends to punish with Claudio's death.

> CLAUDIO: Thus stands it with me. Upon a true contract
> I got possession of Julietta's bed.
> You know the lady; she is fast my wife,
> Save that we do the denunciation lack
> Of outward order. This we came not to,
> Only for propagation of a dower
> Remaining in the coffer of her friends,
> From whom we thought it meet to hide our love
> Till time had made them for us. But it chances
> The stealth of our most mutual entertainment
> With character too gross is writ on Juliet.
> LUCIO: With child, perhaps?
> CLAUDIO: Unhappily, even so. (I, 2, 149–60)

By means of these parallels, Shakespeare suggests a comparison between Claudio and Angelo. In this comparison we cannot help giving Claudio a better grade for morality than Angelo. In one case, there is a rash consummation of marriage between the betrothal and the wedding, which was postponed solely for reasons related to the dowry; in the other case, there is a refusal of marriage between the betrothal and the wedding, again because of the dowry. In his hasty union with Juliet, Claudio certainly acted less badly than Angelo did in his calculated non-acceptance of his union with Mariana.

And so Angelo sleeps with Mariana, whom he takes for the ardently desired Isabella. Then he does something monstrous: contrary to all the promises that he made to Isabella, he nevertheless orders her brother Claudio to be executed the following day. The Duke / Brother Lodowick intervenes, however, and arranges for another man condemned to death to be executed instead of Claudio: Barnardine, a prisoner who is usually drunk, who says, though, that he is not in the mood to die right now. And so finally they send to the governor the head of a pirate who has just died.

When the Duke announces his imminent return and demands that complaints against his deputy, Angelo, be presented as soon as he arrives, Angelo is beset with fears that Isabella might accuse him publicly. Will people believe her or his good reputation? And then he broods over why he had her brother executed: because he was afraid that Claudio's

> riotous youth, with dangerous sense,
> Might in the times to come have ta'en revenge,
> By so receiving a dishonored life
> With ransom of such shame. (IV, 4, 32–35)

Although his panic flares up only briefly, it nevertheless recalls Macbeth and the relentless consequences of his first wicked deed. Angelo's final word before the denouement in the fifth act is like an anti-motto contrasting with the forgiveness at the conclusion:

> Alack, when once our grace we have forgot,
> Nothing goes right. We would, and we would not.
> (IV, 4, 36f.)

One wicked deed draws the next after it. Angelo experiences his entanglement in guilt as unmitigated hopelessness. Yet the light of grace has not been extinguished. The Duke comes back. Isabella begs him for justice and reveals Angelo's guilt, while still thinking that her brother has been executed.

Then Mariana is brought forward. In place of Isabella, she slept with Angelo, and now she is his lawful wedded wife. After further *quid pro quo*, Angelo has no choice but to acknowledge the full extent of his guilt:

O my dread lord,
I should be guiltier than my guiltiness,
To think I can be undiscernible,
When I perceive your Grace, like power divine,
Hath look'd upon my passes. Then, good Prince,
No longer session hold upon my shame,
But let my trial be mine own confession.
Immediate sentence, then, and sequent death,
Is all the grace I beg. (V, 371–79)

The Duke's grace, however, is slower and heavier than a swift death. He sends Angelo off to be married to Mariana. Was that a happy ending?

Then Isabella: Why does the Duke with inhuman cruelty allow her to believe, almost to the very end, that her brother Claudio has been executed? In the logic of the play this is crucial for the theme of pardon. The Duke explains to the newlyweds, Mariana and Angelo, that the mercy of the law demands the death of Angelo:

"An Angelo for Claudio, death for death!"...
Like doth quit like, and measure still for measure.
    (V, 414ff.)

Mariana now begs for Angelo's life. The Duke replies: She should be glad to be a lucky widow with his inheritance. Then Isabella takes the step that, in my estimation, is the high point of the whole play. She kneels down with Mariana and begs forgiveness for Angelo:

Look, if it please you, on this man condemned,
As if my brother lived. I partly think
A due sincerity governed his deeds,
Till he did look on me.... (V, 449ff.)

Since that is so, let him not die! His bad intention, after all, was not carried out.

Her request now to spare him is as unselfish as her rejection of his wicked purpose was resolute. Only now does Angelo fully realize his guilt:

> I am sorry that such sorrow I procure.
> And so deep sticks it in my penitent heart
> That I crave death more willingly than mercy.
> 'Tis my deserving, and I do entreat it. (V, 479ff.)

Only now is it revealed that Claudio lives. And now Angelo is pardoned, too. "I find an apt remission in myself", says the Duke.

And with that everything is ready for the happy ending. Is it one? Every play must end somehow. But is the "pairing off" really so "happy"? For Claudio and Juliet, certainly, but Angelo with Mariana? He should be glad that it ends this way! Lucio, the insolent dandy, remains one to the conclusion: the fact that he must marry the whore he got pregnant is as bad as "pressing to death, whipping, and hanging" (V, 529)—he is cheeky to the last. Finally, Isabella: the Duke's words to her are a marriage proposal. Was she not supposed to enter the convent? Apparently. Does she accept the proposal? We can assume so.

There is no lack of negative commentaries on this conclusion. What about Isabella's zeal for her virginity? Out of the convent and into a princely wedding so quickly? I take the liberty once again to say a word about my own "countercultural" interpretation. I consider Isabella the real heroine of the play. She embodies the stance that shows the true meaning of *mercy and pardon*. In her clear-sightedness, she opposes the moral rigorism of Angelo. Her fidelity to principle is not rigidity or stubbornness, for she knows about human weaknesses. But she is courageous enough to take a stand against the arbitrary tyranny of power. There are moments that allow no compromise, if humanity is to be preserved. This should be clear after the dictatorships of the twentieth century. The climax no doubt is her plea for mercy for Angelo. This can be done only by someone who has personally learned that everything is grace.

Measure for Measure: here the law of "an eye for an eye" no longer applies, but rather a new standard. In the Sermon on the Mount, Jesus said, "Judge not, that you be not judged. For with the judgment you pronounce you will be judged, and the measure you give will be the measure you get" (Mt 7:1–2).

Mercy is the measure with which we will be measured by God. Isabella took her measure from Jesus' measure. I understand why the Duke wants to marry her.